United Nations Economic Commission for Europe

SELF-MADE CITIES

In Search of Sustainable Solutions for Informal Settlements
in the United Nations Economic Commission for Europe Region

UNITED NATIONS
New York and Geneva, 2009

NOTE

Symbols of United Nations documents are composed of capital letters combined with figures. Mention of such a symbol indicates a reference to a United Nations document.

The designations employed and the presentation of the material in this publication do not imply the expression of any opinion whatsoever on the part of the Secretariat of the United Nations concerning the legal status of any country, territory, city or area, or of its authorities, or concerning the delimitation of its frontiers or boundaries.

ECE/HBP/155

UNITED NATIONS PUBLICATIONS
Sales No. E.09.II.E.9
ISBN 978-92-1-117005-4

UNECE Information Service   Phone: +41 (0) 22 917 44 44
Palais des Nations   Fax: +41 (0) 22 917 05 05
CH-1211 Geneva 10   E-mail: info.ece@unece.org
Switzerland   Website: http://www.unece.org

Acknowledgments

Managing team

Team leader: Christina von Schweinichen

Project manager: Paola Deda

Editor: Christopher Edgar

Administrative assistant: Evelina Rioukhina

Authors and contributors

Authors: Sasha Tsenkova, Faculty of Environmental Design, University of Calgary

Contributing authors: Chryssy Potsiou, National Technical University of Athens Anna Badyina, School of Geography and the Environment, University of Oxford

Contributors to boxes: Emanuele Strano, Oxford Institute of Sustainable Development, Oxford Brookes University

Cecilia Serin, Development Studies Institute, London School of Economics and Political Sciences

Layout: Philippe Terrigeol

Cover design: Jakob Krupka

A general thank you to all individuals and organizations that have contributed to this publication with their work and information.

Foreword

More than 50 million people in 15 member States of the United Nation Economic Commission for Europe (UNECE) live in informal settlements. Rapid urbanization, poverty and lack of access to land and ownership, in addition to limited or no social housing, have led citizens to build their homes illegally under very poor environmental and social conditions. The phenomenon is growing at an exponential rate in Eastern Europe, Caucasus and Central Asia, and calls for urgent political, legal and planning solutions.

Over the last 20 years, a number of UNECE countries with economies in transition have had to undertake dramatic policy changes, including land reforms and the massive reallocation of State and private assets.

The economic problems and social stresses related to the transition to new housing and land management systems have added to the many other challenges. In some cases, the lack of a clear and transparent scheme for land tenure and property rights has compounded the problems of already poor administrative and cadastre systems, and hence contributed to the formation of informal settlements.

This study provides a general overview of the phenomenon of informal settlements in the UNECE region and identifies policy responses to address these challenges. Emphasis is given to practices that can facilitate access to affordable land and housing and improve the livelihoods of residents in informal settlements, and in general to strategies that stand to better the physical, social, economic and environmental situation of informal settlements.

The study has four specific objectives:

a. To describe the factors that influence informal settlement development and to define the main characteristics of different types of settlements;

b. To review the major constraints in the existing housing, land management and planning systems that exacerbate the problems of informal settlements, and thus provide an analysis of social, economic and political issues that have a direct influence on the urban development patterns in countries;

c. To provide an overview of the different policy approaches and actions that address the issue of informal settlements which have been implemented at the international, national and local levels, ranging from regularization to upgrading to resettlement;

d. To provide some general guidance that could support decision makers and planners in addressing the challenge of informal settlements.

The analysis here highlights major achievements in addressing the multiple dimensions of informal settlements in cities across the region. The conclusions draw attention to alternatives for local, national and global action and provide guidance on how to face the challenges that informal settlements pose.

This study is the outcome of the joint work of the Committee on Housing and Land Management and the Working Party on Land Administration, which took place in a series of meetings, dedicated workshops and research activities.

I trust that the study will assist policymakers, decision makers, planners and local authorities in their efforts to improve living conditions in informal settlements and/ or find alternative solutions. As the first study of its kind in the region, it is hardly an endpoint for the work on informal settlements by Committee and the Working Party. Rather, it is an initial step towards the development of practical and capacity-building activities in this area, which will facilitate the implementation of sound policies and actions.

Ján Kubiš

Executive Secretary
United Nations Economic Commission for Europe

Preface

I was born in Tirana, my parents too. I thought that living in Tirana city was my privilege, and that everyone, like me, was born there. One day I was walking in the streets of my city with a friend of mine. She came from Kukes, a city in the north-east of Albania. While we were walking, I noticed that she was greeting numerous people in the streets, but I didn't recognize any of them. I realized that Tirana was no longer only mine. Tirana nowadays is for all those that have come from north, south, east and west of Albania. They might not have a house in the centre of Tirana, they might live kilometres away, on the periphery – the so-called "informal areas" – but they work in Tirana. From their homes, spread over thousands of hectares, they flow like streams that join a river and then disappear again into the chaos of the city.

Probably one third of the population lives in informal housing in Albania. Informal settlements occupy 40,000 ha of land, corresponding to approximately 6–8 billion United States dollars worth of investment, considered to be "dead capital". These areas have become satellite cities, described with various terms: "spread cities", "*città diffuse*", "generic cities", "divided cities", "irregular housing", "illegal settlements", "unauthorized housing", "informal developments", etc. The variety of expressions for these informal yet complex solutions pose exciting challenges to researchers, sociologists, economists and politicians.

In the immense expanse of Bathore, Kamza and Paskuqan (three major informal settlements around Tirana), only houses and narrow streets are visible if seen from above; there are no other landmarks, no parks, squares or playgrounds, no shopping centres, schools or kindergartens – only houses and narrow streets, most of which are unpaved. From closer, it looks like a giant dormitory, hosting people at night and bidding them farewell in the early morning: children hand-in-hand with their parents running to the bus station in the main street, others on bicycles, some on motorcycles and cars, all going in one direction – towards Tirana. Owners of shops, restaurants and small businesses, construction workers, hotel workers, street cleaners, waiters, public administrators, mechanics, carpenters – all these informal dwellers invest their work time in the city. They work for the city, but they don't live there. In the morning and late afternoon they commute from the "dormitories" to the city and back. This is the first and most visible impact of these secondary cities that have grown around the big ones. Transit to and from the city is chaotic due to poor road and car conditions and the lack of a proper transportation system, which increases traffic jams, pollution and noise.

They are considered illegal occupants because they have occupied the land illegally, subdivided the land illegally, built illegally and consume water and energy illegally. They work illegally, too.

Last year, I brought my students to one of the informal areas of Tirana: Lapraka, in the proximity of an ex-industrial zone. They were surprised by the size of the houses – much bigger than their city apartments – and by the presence of spacious and green gardens, missing from their city apartments. The houses were surrounded by the high walls and fences that divide two different worlds: the one inside and the one outside. Inside, everything is tidy and well organized; outside, there are open-air sewers, water pipes on top of the sewers, labyrinths of wires accessing electricity from the existing line, and mud or dust covering the narrow streets.

Informal settlements have been the subject of several studies and projects, yet a number of questions remain unanswered. How is it possible that people can obtain illegally what is not accessible through legal means? Should these "secondary cities" be ignored, or should the problems they pose be addressed? Should these settlements be demolished or legalized?

The phenomenon is so complex that solutions cannot be generic and comprehensive.

This UNECE study will provide you with some of the tools necessary to address the problems related to informal settlements. It shows, for the first time, that the problem of informal housing is not typical only of poor countries, but affects many UNECE member States as well and can be exacerbated by the bureaucratic procedures that exist even in wealthier European Union countries. The study will add value to the work so far undertaken in the subregion of South-Eastern Europe and will highlight the efforts of some Governments to address the difficulties and challenges related to informal settlements.

Doris Andoni

Chairperson
Committee on Housing and Land Management
United Nations Economic Commission for Europe

This publication describes and elaborates on the phenomenon of illegal settlements in the UNECE region that came into being for a number of reasons, including poverty and the search for shelter and labour opportunities.

The more one goes through the study, the more worrisome and at the same time challenging the subject becomes. Worrisome, because the size and geographical extension of the problem of unplanned or illegal development and its consequences for the lives of so many people in the region becomes evident. Challenging, because it is very clear from the outset that there is no "one-size-fits-all" solution when it comes to informal settlements.

This study cannot address the numerous different realities, but it does show, despite the very different circumstances in the countries across the UNECE region, that there are common goals and approaches targeted at the improvement of the current situation. It also identifies a number of tools addressing spatial planning and the legalization of informal settlements and social housing, to either mitigate existing problems or prevent informal developments whenever possible.

UNECE has been addressing with the establishment and maintenance of land administration systems since the early 1990s, when many countries of the region started a transition process towards market-oriented economies. As land administrations, current and accurate spatial information on land and healthy land markets are of vital importance for sustainable spatial planning and development, this study assumes a certain urgency from the perspective of land administration. Of critical importance in this context are well-balanced land policies developed within the framework of good governance, including land management strategies and formal property or tenure rights. These will enable planning and sustainable development at the national, regional or local levels.

The study shows that it is necessary to approach the issue of informal development in a integrated manner, one that involves various disciplines and perspectives and includes both urban infrastructure and rural areas. As solving the problem of informal settlements supports the achievement of the United Nations Millennium Development Goals of poverty eradication and environmental sustainability, UNECE will closely follow the issue in the future and will continue to bring the perspectives of land management to the attention of policymakers.

I trust that this study will reach policymakers and stakeholders operating in planning, land-use management and regional development. I strongly believe that it will substantially contribute to raising awareness of the challenges posed by informal settlements, and will enable policy dialogue and promote sustainable land use across the UNECE region.

Peter Creuzer

Chairman
Working Party on Land Administration
United Nations Economic Commission for Europe

Table of Contents

List of figures, tables and boxes

Acronyms

EECCA: Eastern Europe, Caucasus and Central Asia
IDPs: Internally displaced persons
NGO: Non-governmental organization
UNECE: United Nations Economic Commission for Europe
UN-HABITAT: United Nations Human Settlements Programme
UNHCR: United Nations High Commissioner for Refugees

Executive Summary

The purpose of this study is to provide a general overview of the phenomenon of informal settlements in the UNECE region, to identify policy responses to address these challenges and to highlight results achieved. Emphasis is given to practices that can facilitate access to affordable land and housing and improve the livelihoods of residents in informal settlements, and in general to strategies that can better the physical, social, economic and environmental situation of informal settlements.

THE PROBLEM

The study has revealed that the problem is significant in more than 20 countries in the UNECE region and affects the lives of over 50 million people. The critical factors affecting the formation of informal settlements are related to several major interrelated changes: (a) rapid urbanization and influx of people into select urban areas; (b) unrealistic or insufficient planning regulations and inefficient land administration; (c) wars and natural disasters leading to the massive movement of people to places of opportunity and safety; and (d) poverty and the lack of low cost housing and serviced land.

In particular, poverty and social exclusion are key drivers of the formation of illegal settlements in most countries. While public expenditure for subsidized housing and urban rehabilitation is spiraling downward, the need to address the social and economic challenges in these areas is growing. Furthermore, pressure to reduce government deficits and redirect spending priorities towards more productive sectors of the economy also influence the ability of different countries to undertake comprehensive measures to address informal settlements. As a result, even Western European countries have about six per cent of their urban dwellers living in extremely precarious conditions, often in rundown inner-city areas, which are not necessarily illegal but which exhibit poverty, social exclusion and housing deprivation. In low-income countries in particular, high unemployment, poverty and social polarization adversely affect people's ability to house themselves.

Inadequate housing is a central issue for informal settlements and is thus essential to introducing sustainable housing policy. However, a narrow technical understanding of housing policy cannot provide a comprehensive framework to tackle the multiple problems of informal settlements; the complex relationships between housing and other aspects of human life must be clearly understood and a broader role of housing policy in addressing disadvantages of informal settlements should be developed. There is generally a need for a new concept of housing policy. Such a policy must be committed to social equity and to improving the standards of living of disadvantaged groups.

Social inequality needs to be seen as an obstacle to sustainable urban development and to cities successfully competing in the local and global arenas. Social justice must be a central item on the holistic housing policy agenda and a precondition for sustainable urban development. One of the necessary approaches is to make housing policy an effective mechanism in accumulating asset wealth for the poor, through ensuring equal access and securing rights to the resources essential to supporting a decent life.

EXISTING POLICY FRAMEWORK

The challenge of informal settlements is widely recognized in international and national sustainable development programmes. There have been a number of important policies documents related to the issue of informal settlements both globally and in the UNECE region including the Global Strategy for Shelter to the Year 2000 and the Millennium Development Goals established by the United Nations Millennium Declaration in 2000. For example, upgrading informal settlements is critical step on the path to achieving its target 4 for Goal 7 (by 2020, to have achieved a significant improvement in the lives of at least 100 million slum dwellers).

In translating the Millennium Development Goals into the context of the UNECE region, a special UNECE report provided a comprehensive framework that includes the following key clusters: (a) an enabling environment for pro-poor and sustained growth; (b) the equity issue; (c) distribution of assets and opportunities, d) distribution of income and social protection; (e) fostering employment and promoting human capital; (f) an enabling external environments; and (g) environmental sustainability (UNECE, 2006).

The Vienna Declaration on National and Regional Policy Programmes regarding Informal Settlements in South-Eastern Europe[1] established the general characteristics of informal settlements while also taking account of the diversity of the phenomenon in different national contexts. The need to tackle informal settlements in a sustainable way and to prevent their future growth has also been recognized. This is based on a

---

[1] South-Eastern Europe typically includes the following countries: Albania, Bosnia and Herzogovina, Croatia, Greece, Kosovo (Serbia), Montenegro, Serbia and the former Yugoslav Republic of Macedonia.

better understanding of the right of each urban citizen to be an equal member of the community. A new commitment with respect to "sustainable urban management, good governance, urban social and economic integration of informal settlements within the overall city structure" has been made. The Vienna Declaration highlighted the need for an adequate legal and institutional environment and invited effective policies and programmes to regularize informal settlements in a sustainable way by the year 2015 (Vienna Declaration, 2004).

In 2006, the UNECE Committee on Housing and Land Management adopted the Ministerial Declaration on Social and Economic Changes in Distressed Urban Areas. This Declaration promotes the provision of adequate housing and identifies the improvement of informal settlements as a main priority. In in-depth discussions in 2007, the Committee emphasized the need for a comprehensive approach across the UNECE region that would integrate urban planning, housing and land management policies (ECE/HBP/2007/7, ECE/HBP/WP.7/2007/8).

KEY FINDINGS

Types of informal settlements and policy approaches

Informal settlements include the following types: (a) squatter settlements on public or private land; (b) settlements for refugees and vulnerable people; (c) upgraded squatter settlements; (d) illegal suburban land subdivisions on private or public land, often on the urban fringe; and (e) overcrowded, dilapidated housing without adequate facilities, in city centres or densely urbanized areas.

Many countries in the region have attempted to address the challenges of informal settlements in the last few decades through control over territorial development, land management and more systematic building inspection. The search for policy solutions to address illegal settlements has been multi-faceted and multi-dimensional. Various projects and urban development programmes have been implemented in countries such as Greece, Italy, Portugal and Spain in the last 20 years. Although current needs may differ, these countries can be an important source of good practices for others in the UNECE region facing similar challenges. In some transition countries, with a recent rise of the intensity of the phenomenon, efforts have focused on the general improvement of land registration systems and property cadastre to allow more effective land policy implementation. While these measures have not explicitly targeted the problem of informal settlements, they have generally provided a better foundation for urban planning, land management and building regulations.

The following major types of policy interventions are reviewed in the report: (a) legalization; (b) regularization and upgrading; (c) the development of alternative housing systems; (d) resettlement and reallocation; and (e) addressing the challenges of substandard inner-city housing.

Drivers of change

In general, the problems of informal settlements have not been systematically addressed and responsibilities remain fragmented. Informal settlements and residents have often been neglected in broader urban and social development practices. Some communities in informal settlements have opted for self-organization, these initiatives often being backed by the media, local government, international organizations and non-governmental organizations (NGOs). Even if these cases are limited, the process of self-organization has had many positive outcomes. Currently, however, there is a global call for urgent yet sustainable interventions vis-à-vis informal settlements. Governments are translating relevant global strategies into specific national contexts. Higher-level government is increasingly seen as key enabler of change. There is also a commitment to ensure equal access to basic human rights as well as fairness in wealth redistribution. Public-private partnerships are often at the centre of decision-making. A strong tendency towards mobilizing local skills and knowledge can also be noticed.

Successful interventions

As it has been mentioned, various urban development projects have been undertaken in the last 20 years. The solutions range from legalization and regularization to the provision of essential social and engineering infrastructure, to resettlement programmes in social housing and to inclusion in formal urban planning. It has become evident that it is only through adopting comprehensive integrated solutions that better outcomes of informal settlement interventions can be achieved. Successful responses should be based on acknowledging the varied forces behind different types of informal settlements and the need to apply a range of policy tools (social, economic, spatial planning) simultaneously. For such integration to be effective, responses must be framed by long-term strategies to achieve wider societal goals based on the principles of sustainability and social fairness. Equal, affordable and safe access to such basic human rights as land and shelter are the preconditions for the development of sustainable places and communities.

Obstacles

A number of problems have prevented existing programmes for informal settlements from achieving successful outcomes. Insufficient financial and human resources, burdensome regulatory rules, unclear administrative procedures and unrealistic standards have all been reported as major barriers. In some cases, responses have been reactive and hostile rather than comprehensive, strategic and proactive. The failure of many programmes can be attributed to a misunderstanding of the deeper causes underlying the formation of informal settlements, e.g. social inequality and unequal redistribution of wealth, as well as to a limited application of such policy tools as integrated land management, e.g. land administration (multi-purpose cadastre) and spatial planning. Land administration and spatial planning are fundamental land tools and they should be used in coordination to each other to achieve the best results.

Responses to the housing question often remain very technical and the development of the housing sector has not been given the priority it deserves within the context of national economic and social development. The proper coordination between housing policy and other policies has yet to be developed.

An enabling environment for the market to work efficiently is also lacking in several countries. In these countries, it has to operate within an obsolete legal and policy framework and administrative structure.

The belief in the market as a one-size-fits-all solution often further marginalizes alternative developments and reinforces the problems of informal settlements, especially when applied in countries with a general legal framework for land development and a relevant administrative structure that reflect the land policies and practices of the previous century.

Lessons for policy consideration

It is important to consider a number of important initiatives when translating the informal settlements agenda into local contexts. Better outcomes have been possible because of:

a. Changes in policymaking towards a strategic vision and planning for short-, medium- and long-term solutions;

b. Creation of an effective governance framework that comprises key actors across different fields and empowers voices of marginalized groups;

c. Establishment of a platform for a dialogue between key actors, as well as effective public-private partnerships;

d. A willingness to draw on existing practices and learn from other experiences to support the policy process, and an eagerness for continuous learning and knowledge-sharing;

e. A new commitment to fighting social inequality and establishing social justice and transparency;

f. A thorough analysis of the major causes affecting residents' living conditions;

g. Establishment of efficient linkages between major land tools for land management, e.g. housing, land administration and spatial planning;

h. Development of urban strategies that focus on the settlement level but taking due account of the importance of the settlement's connection to broader social, economic, environmental and urban development processes.

RECOMMENDATIONS AND KEY PRINCIPLES

1. Based on the study, the following key policy principles are proposed to guide informal settlement interventions:

2. There is no "one-size-fits-all" solution to address the problems of informal settlements and the choice of policy tools should be comprehensive and should consider the specific socio-cultural context.

3. Policies to address informal settlements must be based on the understanding that they are spatial manifestations of social inequality and on a comprehension of the complex and multidimensional nature of social inequality. Effective responses to multiple disadvantages within informal settlements should integrate different social-supporting measures.

4. The adoption of an integrated national strategy to address social inequality and unequal spatial redistribution of wealth is fundamental to better policy outcomes for informal settlements.

5. Joint and inclusive approaches to governance would ensure better results in relation to informal settlements interventions.

6. Strategies for informal settlements must be based on a clear understanding of the nature of deprivation and should pursue an integrated, people-focused and place-based approach.

7. Housing, land and spatial planning policies must always be a key focus for informal settlement policy interventions, and should constitute part of an integrated national strategy to address poverty reduction and general economic development.

8. It is important to formulate a national strategy for housing that supports marginalized communities.

9. Informal settlements must be part of a well-designed system of land management committed to providing people with affordable access to serviced land.

10. There must exist a pro-poor spatial planning system based on the principles of sustainable development.

11. People's knowledge and access to information should be improved.

12. Spatial planning and zoning regulation are necessary. Recording of land uses should be made transparent and available to all.

13. Urban administration policies should meet current social, environmental and economic needs.

Methodology and references

This analytical assessment is based on existing information from government reports and draws on comparative evaluations on the topic carried out by major international organizations such as the Office of the United Nations High Commissioner for Refugees (UNHCR), the United Nations Human Settlements Programme (UN-HABITAT), the World Bank (Europe and Central Asia) and international research institutes. It also draws information from the UNECE country housing profiles and land administration reviews, as well as statistics from officially published sources of information and international databases. Papers presented at FIG[2] Commission 3/ UNECE workshop on informal settlements ("Spatial Information Management: Towards Legalizing Informal Urban Development", 2007) were particularly helpful to the author in highlighting the different approaches in the region.

In addition to secondary sources of information, a special survey was designed by the UNECE secretariat and sent to over 50 government officials and policy experts representing the countries taking part in the UNECE Committee on Housing and Land Management and Working Party on Land Administration. A list of countries where there are significant informal settlement challenges and/or programmes was created. The survey collected information on several important themes:

a. The phenomenon of informal settlement development: the quantitative and qualitative assessment and factors affecting the process (e.g. limitations in the planning system, land administration and access to affordable housing);

b. Policy approaches and strategies to address the problems (e.g. legal acts that regularize and upgrade informal settlements, and the city or national programmes in place);

c. Case studies of successful intervention and good practices with an emphasis on results achieved.

It is important to note that both the survey and this study do not focus on problems of illegal construction, e.g. additions, illegal changes to existing legal buildings and other modifications that exceed building or planning permits. The emphasis here is on clusters of illegal developments establishing informal settlement patterns and neighbourhoods.

---

[2] International Federation of Surveyors.

Introduction

Informal Settlements: A Complex Phenomenon

Informal settlements are often characterized as "illegal" residential formations lacking basic infrastructure, security of tenure, adequate housing, etc. However such an interpretation is only the tip of the iceberg, underneath which lay the various and complex socio-cultural processes that lead to informal settlements' formation. In order to evaluate the phenomenon, it is therefore necessary to analyze the underlying socio-cultural context.

Informal settlements have always been a persistent feature of urbanization. Recent economic changes within the UNECE region and the break-up of the Soviet Union in particular resulted in welfare state retrenchment, the privatization of public responsibilities and the commodification of different sectors. Such major administrative and economic reforms were not accompanied by necessary contemporary land administration tools, e.g. efficient legislation and legal reform, appropriate land valuation, property taxation, measures for smooth economic development within the countries, transparency in land development procedures and real estate markets, and updated land administration and planning regulations. Related economic problems such as the lack of sustainable policies for creating jobs and reducing unemployment, as well as inefficient banking systems for mortgage lending in many Eastern European countries and lack of social housing policy, have resulted in dispossession and impoverishment of large strata of the population and growing socio-economic disparities. Soaring social inequalities have had a significant impact on the spatial patterns of cities, whose populations have found themselves trapped by a chronic lack of the necessary resources for adequate housing. Regardless of the type, settlements built with poor security of land tenure and without any planning regulations or building controls are considered as informal and need upgrading. Similar examples can be found worldwide.

The negative spatial manifestation of informal settlements can be either reinforced by inappropriate policies or successfully mitigated through proactive policies. A limited understanding of the problems of informal settlements raises the risk of failure to achieve the intended results.

Informal settlements are mainly viewed through the perspective of "housing problems". Indeed, the development of proactive housing policy should be considered as a key element in informal settlement transformation. Housing policy, however, should be considered comprehensively and not in narrow technical definitions. The complex relationships between housing and other aspects of human life must be clearly understood and a broader role of housing policy in addressing disadvantages of informal settlements should be developed. There is a general need to design new concepts in housing policy. Social justice must be a major factor and a precondition for sustainable urban development. A necessity is to make housing policy an effective mechanism in accumulating asset wealth for the dispossessed, through ensuring equal access to the rights to land and resources essential to leading a decent life.

CHAPTER 1

Informal Settlements in the United Nations Economic Commission for Europe Region

1. Informal settlements and the global agenda

The challenge of informal settlements is widely recognized in international and national programmes fostering sustainable development. The second United Nations Conference on Human Settlements (Habitat II, Istanbul, Turkey, 3–14 June 1996) was a key historical moment signaling a new pathway for long-term policy development. A comprehensive vision and broad policy agendas previously endorsed by the New Urban Agenda and the Global Strategy for Shelter were reaffirmed. Furthermore, chapter 7 of Agenda 21 introduced the idea of sustainable development in application to human settlements. This signaled a transition from fragmented policy responses towards a more comprehensive policy agenda.

The UN-Habitat Agenda adopted in 1996 and the Declaration on Cities and Other Human Settlements in the New Millennium adopted by a special session of the United Nations General Assembly in 2001 reaffirmed the commitment of Governments to ensure that "Everyone will have adequate shelter that is healthy, safe, secure, accessible and affordable and that includes basic services, facilities and amenities, and will enjoy freedom from discrimination in housing and legal security of tenure" (UN Habitat, 2001). To achieve this fundamental goal an emphasis was placed on collaboration between public and private actors and institutions, as well as the identification of "enabling strategies".

Within the UNECE region, the Council of Europe has emphasized the importance of the "enabling framework" for housing policies of European Union (EU) Member States. In the Revised European Social Charter of 1996 (Art 31), a more concrete commitment is advocated: "With a view to ensuring the effective exercise of the right to housing, the Parties undertake to take measures designed: to promote access to housing of an adequate standard; to prevent and reduce homelessness with a view to its gradual elimination; to make the price of housing accessible to those without adequate resources". Furthermore, the Charter of Fundamental Rights of the European Union of 2000 acknowledges the right to property, social security and social assistance. According to its article 34.3: "In order to combat social exclusion and poverty, the Union recognizes and respects the right to social and housing assistance so as to ensure a decent existence for all those who lack sufficient resources".

In this context, the UNECE Committee on Housing and Land Management adopted a Ministerial Declaration on Social and Economic Changes in Distressed Urban Areas (2006) to promote the provision of adequate housing, and identified the improvement of informal settlements as a priority. In recent in-depth discussions, the Committee emphasized the need for a comprehensive approach across the UNECE region, integrating urban planning, housing and land management policies (ECE/HBP/2007/7, ECE/HBP/WP.7/2007/8).

On the subregional level, the Vienna Declaration on National and Regional Policy Programmes on Informal Settlements in South-Eastern Europe identifies the issue as a priority and invites policies to legalize and improve informal settlements in a sustainable way. It argues that the prevention of future settlements' formation is critical through sustainable urban management, principles of good governance and capacity-building (Vienna Declaration, 2004).[3] In response to the global call for action, Governments in the UNECE region have developed action plans and various programmes to address informal settlements while recognizing the diversity of housing and land management systems, including land administration in different countries.

The United Nations, along with its subsidiary bodies and other international organizations, acknowledges and recognizes secure tenure of housing as a fundamental human right. Addressing the challenge of informal settlements is also critical for the achievement of the Millennium Development Goals, particularly Target 11 on slums. Insufficient social and physical infrastructure and the lack of government involvement to improve the conditions in some informal housing settlements are the driving forces that contribute to extreme poverty, higher child mortality and deteriorating urban conditions (UN-HABITAT, 2003).

In line with the principles of international agendas, this study builds upon the fundamental human right to adequate housing, adequate legal and institutional framewortks and, thus, to credit and economic improvement.

---

[3] In the effort to help Albania, Bosnia and Herzegovina, Croatia, Kosovo (Serbia), Montenegro, Serbia and the former Yugoslav Republic of Macedonia meet their Vienna Declaration commitments and improve their performance in the human settlements sector, the Stability Pact and UN-HABITAT joined forces and initiated a "Regional Capacity Strengthening Programme for Urban Development and Housing (RCSP)", which is currently in its demonstration phase.

2. Typology and formation processes

Given the significant regional diversity of informal settlements, and hence different understandings behind the definition of "informal settlement", it is necessary to avoid seeing such a complex phenomenon as two-dimensional (formal/or informal) only. It is multidimensional nature and the whole spectrum of formality/informality that should be taken into consideration. What is also required for better policy outcomes is the development of a broader understanding of informal settlement formations.

At least two conceptualizations have usually been applied in discussions about informal settlements: they may be defined as the narrow and broad understandings of the informal settlements phenomenon. A narrow understanding is when the consideration of informal settlements is dominated by the images from the Third World, poverty and self-made housing areas. In particular, post-Soviet transition countries have limited knowledge of informal settlements, because housing in the Soviet era was considered as a universal right, with the State providing housing and basic infrastructure free-of-charge and centrally. With the commodification of access to housing and facilities in these countries, residents have been experiencing degraded standards of living, which also now represent a great challenge for policymakers. This is why it is important to raise awareness and to develop a broad understanding of the phenomenon as well as to suggest possible solutions. This study promotes a broader understanding of the phenomenon of informal settlements in the member countries; it considers informal settlements as certain living conditions and that their spatial manifestation does not conform to formal rules, standards and institutions.

Based on the findings from the case studies, a typology of informal settlements has been created (table 1). This typology is based on the generally agreed characteristics (conditions) of informal settlements formations (e.g. informal/formal legal status, secure/insecure tenure, bad/good physical conditions, access to basic infrastructure, and safe/unsafe environment). Whether a given settlement/housing development is formal or informal is judged based on the agreed characteristics, each representing two opposite states (formal/informal, secure/insecure, etc.); however, it is not these opposite states of each of the characteristics that are brought into consideration, but rather the whole spectrum between them (see the typology graphs on the spectrum of characteristics). Furthermore, the typology also includes other crucial characteristics that have not usually been recognized, but that have shaped the quality of life in informal settlements, namely socio-cultural, economic and political conditions. If policy responses are to be effective and committed to sustainability, they should look beyond the generally agreed characteristics to understand such deeper socio-cultural, economic and political effects (see the typology graph on the spectrum of policy responses). Effective outcomes of policy interventions to improve informal settlements will depend on such deeper understanding of the phenomenon.

Table 1: Typology of informal settlements

N	The formal/informal continuum	Distinctive characteristics	Operational sub-categories
1	*De jure:* Illegal land occupation, informal housing with no planning permits, not integrated into a broader urban system *De facto:* Relatively good living standards, tolerated (recognized)	Secure tenure, relatively good quality residential developments, good access to infrastructure; in some cases integration into master plans could be achieved over time, located in city centres or peri-urban areas; in some cases evolved into established vibrant neighbourhoods with viable rental and homeownership markets	Upgraded "squatter" settlements
2	*De jure:* legal title to, but illegal subdivisions of suburban land, housing with no planning permits, built in violation of land use plans, building standards *De facto:* Tolerated, relatively good housing, commodified and used by developers to provide housing to middle class families **Can also include:** *De jure:* Occupation of urban land with unclear legal status, housing built in violation of established regulations *De facto:* Good housing conditions to provide housing to upper-middle class families; may be approved but in most cases is contested	Good-quality housing (in some cases luxurious) and access to infrastructure, dwellings are not only owner-occupied, but include a vibrant commercial rental housing sector, controlled by individual homeowners and by speculative developers	Unauthorized land developments or illegal subdivisions on the fringes of cities in South-Eastern Europe—from Serbia to Bosnia and Herzegovina and Greece Extra-urban settlements in protected or recreation zones and coastal areas Unauthorized Infill housing constructions in cities

N	The formal/informal continuum	Distinctive characteristics	Operational sub-categories
3	*De jure:* Temporary legal residence *De facto:* Unacceptable living standards	Settlements, although newer, often present extremely poor living conditions, generally found in the urban periphery, in pockets of marginal land, or close to collective centres for refugees	Temporary housing/settlements for refugees Temporary structures, domiki, small caravans set up in public places. Dormitories and damaged unsafe housing as temporary shelter for refugees Former hotels, schools and kindergartens converted to temporary housing
4	*De jure:* Formal residential areas developed on public or private land *De facto:* Inadequate housing condition (not meet minimum living standards)	Degraded or unsafe physical conditions, unhealthy or overcrowded living conditions (subdivision of apartments, shared facilities), poor access to infrastructure, obsolete technical systems, location in urban or peripheral areas; secure tenure might be a problem, occupation by homeowners/tenants with weak economic and political status, or, in some cases, by illegal migrants	Degrading multi-family housing stock (includes private as well as public housing stock) Housing stock below safety standards Illegal use of basements and attics of multi-family houses to accommodate illegal migrants Overcrowded housing (inadequate living space for a growing family) Deprived inner-city neighborhoods with slum-like conditions originally developed as planned areas with high concentration of low-income groups
5	*De jure:* Illegally occupied private or public land, spontaneous housing *De facto:* Threat of eviction, demolition, multiple exclusion, self-help response to limited access to housing	Self-built substandard housing units often lack basic necessities, sanitation and running water (slums), can grow towards complex, organized settlements, located in peri-urban areas and on public or private land	Squatter settlements (e.g. shanty towns, peri-urban settlements and slums, *baracas, favelas, bidonvilles, gecekondu, chabolas*) Smaller pockets of informal housing built illegally under bridges and overpasses, and on vacant plots of land close to industrial zones and railway reserves, river banks, landslides, waste dumps and landfill sites

In general, despite a great range of spatial manifestations across the UNECE region, there are several major types of informal settlements:

a.   Squatter settlements on public or private land;

b.   Settlements for refugees and vulnerable people;

c.   Upgraded squatter settlements;

d.   Illegal suburban land subdivisions on legally owned private, with illegal changing of land-use regulations, often on the urban fringe;

e.   Overcrowded, dilapidated housing without adequate facilities in city centers or densely urbanized areas.

In different ways, all five types of informal settlements accommodate mainly the needs of the urban poor or low-income and other disadvantaged groups, and exacerbate their poverty. In several countries across the region, the formation of informal settlements is not new but dates back to the 1950s and 1960s. Particularly, in Greece Italy and Portugal, internal or external migrations have significantly contributed to the urbanization processes. Moreover, in some cases, other reasons – such as unrealistic regulations rather than poverty – have led to certain forms of informal construction along coastlines and in holiday areas. In countries in Western and Southern Europe, informal settlements are also due to the new waves of massive migration, caused by poor economic situations in countries in transition and post-conflict areas.

In others, the informal settlements are fairly recent, but have become the dominant form of urban growth in the 1990s. It is important to note that in some cases, residents of some informal settlements are not necessarily poor; rather, the informality of the development is used as the only way to overcome existing complex and time-consuming planning and long delays in expanding of city plans and development permitting procedures as well as unrealistic land management constraints. Of course, there are cases where both individuals and developers have built housing with speculative purposes, without any planning or building permit but on privately owned land acquired through legal means. In other words, many manifestations of informal settlements across the region invoke images of poverty, exclusion and despair, but there are certainly examples where this is not the case. These processes producing different types of informal settlements should be well analysed, as different, corresponding policy approaches might be necessary.

International literature also has useful examples to provide – for example, of housing policies developed to support slum dwellers, by definition poor, that have failed simply because of the profit-oriented nature of the settlers, who are willing to sell the houses offered to them by the State, use the money to cover other needs, and then go back to live in slums where the rest of their relatives live. All these cases, and the experience gained from other countries, should be taken into consideration when adopting policies to tackle the phenomenon of informal settlements.

A. Upgraded squatter settlements

Within the informal settlements across the region, there is a great variety of settlement patterns and historic circumstances. Some that started as squatter settlements in the peri-urban areas in the 1960s (in Greece, Turkey and parts of the former Yugoslavia) have evolved into more established neighborhoods. Skopje, for example, has 27 illegally constructed neighbourhoods dating back to the earthquake in the 1980s.

There is a risk that under such regeneration programmes priority may be given to physical upgrading, with the result that other aspects important for "improving living conditions" are neglected. It is essential to provide security of tenure and to deliver the integration of informal settlements into the broader urban structure and society. There is a great risk for marginalized people to be displaced either physically or by market forces if a neighborhood regeneration strategy is isolated from complementary policies.

On the other hand, there is evidence that a legalization process based on recognition of freehold rights does not work either. These policies usually succeed in so far as services become upgraded in informal settlement, but there is little evidence that legalization of land rights actually takes place. Even if such policies achieve individual security of tenure, they fail to integrate people and places into the broader urban structure and society.

It is the legalization of housing rights that grants legal security of tenure, ensures socio-spatial integration of people and communities and assures the rights of people to stay in places after the transformation process. Recent regularization practices have shown that alongside an effective system of tenure security, it is very important to recognize the rights to adequate and affordable housing, especially for marginalized groups. It is not simply individual property rights to which housing rights are related. A number of sustainable programmes that integrate both upgrading and legalization have recently been reported. An integrated approach is argued to control both formal and informal land markets. In this way, it is the residents of informal settlements who will benefit from public investment, rather than the property developers or other interests who do not fulfill their commitment to providing people with adequate and affordable housing.

In Belgrade, informal settlements occupy 22 per cent of the land for construction (see box 1), and in Istanbul, 70 per cent of the population lives in informal housing (*gecekondu*). Variety also exists in the legal status of these settlements: while most begin with an illegal occupation of land, over time some security of tenure is acquired with a formally recognized legal title of land (e.g. in Serbia, and the former Yugoslav Republic of Macedonia). In the case of Greece, the legal status in the majority of cases was not squatting but full ownership of illegal sub-divided rural land, which over the years was formally recognized. Due to various overlapping regulations and non-compliance with planning norms, residents often lack planning permits.

Over time, de facto legality is implied by the fact that the settlements are not demolished, (due to the lack of affordable housing policy), and that some infrastructure, e.g. road networks, public transportation, piped water, electricity and sewer, space for common use, etc, has been gradually provided (e.g. projects in Ankara, illegal connections in Serbia, and in most cases in Greece). There are cases where these settlements are included in the new master plans of cities, recognizing their alternative development standards. Since the 1970s, tolerance towards squatter settlements has grown and the numbers of forced evictions and demolitions have diminished. This has enabled some of the more established settlements to develop rapidly, with residents investing in their homes and improving the local environment. These upgraded settlements are often vibrant neighborhoods with viable rental and homeownership markets. In some of the Turkish *gecekondu* in Ankara and Istanbul, studies underline a pattern of commodification, manifested in the replacement of older homes with multi-storey, multi-family structures capitalizing on land values and locational advantages (Carley 2001, Devecigil 2005).

Box 1: Upgrading informal settlements: Kalugerica, Serbia

Kaluderica is one of the fastest growing settlements in Serbia and arguably the largest village in the Balkans. Located just 8 km away from Belgrade, it has grown rapidly together with the city since the 1980s when it was home to 12,000 people. Its population today is estimated at 50,000, accommodating the influx of the refugees from Bosnia and Herzegovina, Croatia and Kosovo (Serbia). Although officially classified as a rural settlement, five times the size of its municipal seat Grocka, Kalugerica is a city built by its residents in an informal way. Most of the houses do not have a building permit, but the residents own the land and it might be even registered in the cadastre. Over time, people have negotiated connections to infrastructure, built roads and arranged for services by Belgrade's City Public Transportation Company and Telekom Serbia.

Source: *Belgrade Master Plan*

Box 2: City profile: Milan, Italy

Those urban areas characterized by self-construction began to be called 'Koreas' due to their visual similarity with images coming from the Korean War (Foot 2005)

After the Second World War, Italy experienced massive flows of domestic migration: whole families left the poorer areas of the country to escape the widespread unemployment affecting many Italian regions at the time.

In the metropolitan area of Milan, the population increased by 26 per cent between 1951 and 1971 (600,000 people in 20 years). This influx heavily impacted the city. Coming from the south and north-east of Italy, and from the islands as well as from other areas of Lombardy, immigrants faced difficulties in finding affordable shelter in Milan, and settled in municipalities located in Milan's immediate surroundings.

Often immigrants settled further from urban centres, in the countryside, both for economic (the price of urban accommodation was unaffordable) and social (easier integration with the rural population) reasons.

This was the beginning of the "Koreas", self-built urban villages located in the countryside around the major urban centre starting the early 1950s. Such settlements were characterized by small, single-family detached houses in small lots of different shapes, without any formal organization, and in dense but dispersed aggregations. In a few decades, small hamlets grew into urban settlements. For instance, in Bollate, in north Milan, the population increased fourfold (from 9,625 to 42,770 between 1936 and 1971) and the population of "Villaggio dei Giovi" in Limbiate, also in north Milan – one of the largest Korean settlements – skyrocketed from 10 in 1945 to 13,000 in 1980.

The history of Korean settlements can be portrayed as a four-step process:

1. Early phase. First houses were built on legally purchased lots and settlements grew around old pre-existing farmhouses or rural nuclei, with a chronic lack of all basic infrastructures (e.g. sewerage, electricity, streets).

2. Development phase. Settlements rapidly expanded: the original small houses quickly became larger and the settlement became more articulated, around straight streets, forming spontaneous aggregations. The social hierarchy was fundamental to this development. Many "older Korean" inhabitants rented parts of their houses to newcomers to support additions and enlargements. Supporting networks of entrepreneurs, professionals and real estate developers offered their services to the Koreas. Municipalities finally became aware of the problem and began providing technical and service infrastructure to the new settlements. Building permissions were secured relatively easily, as the only requirements for buildings and lots to be legalized were the existence of "straight streets" and "hygienic standards".

3. Consolidation phase. Houses were rearranged and enlarged thanks to new waves of immigration that increased the number of inhabitants. The original settlers, now landlords, moved to wealthier areas or to the upper floors of their houses, renting underutilized rooms (e.g. canteens, garages and ground floors). In this phase, Koreas exhibited the capacity to generate commercial and retail activities, reaching a higher level of self-sufficiency. Telephone, street, electricity and sewage networks were also in place.

4. Ageing phase. In this current phase, beginning in the late 1980s and 1990s, the average population is perceptibly older, as younger generations have often moved away and new immigrants have arrived from other countries. The local network of retail and services has been wiped out by large commercial malls, which have cropped up everywhere in the expanding urban fringe.

Bollate municipality, formed 50 years ago, is an interesting case study of a Korea settlement. The area was favoured by immigration flows after the Second World War, due to the advantageous conditions and its strategic position, located close to with Milan's industrial districts.

First Korean settlements in Bollate developed around two small rural settlements: Cassina del Sole and Cassina Nuova. The first Korea, named St. Giuseppe, started in 1951 on the initiative of immigrants from the Veneto region. The community took off in 1953 with the first wave of new immigrants from the south of Italy, with the most intense phase of construction taking place between 1956 and 1960.

The southern part of the Korea started a bit later, when a first settlement was built in 1954, also by Veneti, not far from the Korea of St. Giuseppe. This new settlement began growing intensively in 1956 when, again, new immigrants from the south colonized all the undeveloped land. The local press began acknowledging the Koreas existence, with some delay, in 1961.

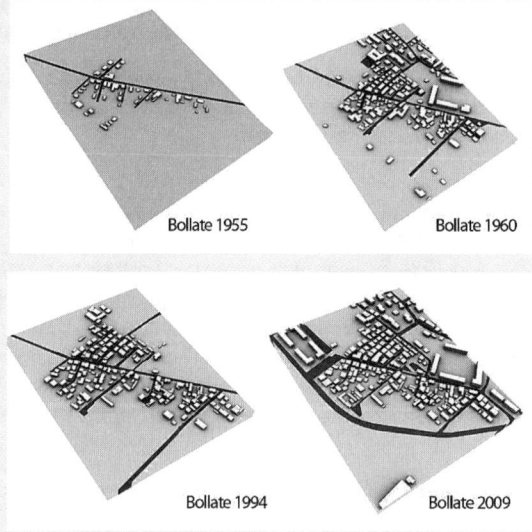

Bollate 1955   Bollate 1960

Bollate 1994   Bollate 2009

Development of Bollate between 1955 and 2009

During this period, in Milan social housing interventions were pursued in many suburbs to deal with further formation of informal settlements and to provide a more suitable housing solution for the immigrants. One of these large social housing complexes followed a project of a rather well-known Italian architect.

A few kilometres from the Korea "Sud" settlement, in Bollate, the complex is a single 600 m², five-storey building with 160 dwellings served by eight external stairwells. As in the Koreas, this complex is mainly inhabited by elderly and new foreign immigrants (many of them illegal). Their living conditions here are very hard, and are considered to be much worse than those of self-organized Koreas. Single elderly people must live in dwellings that are too large for them. The buildings are extremely downgraded and in a bad structural state. As tenants of the Social Housing Agency that owns the complex, inhabitants live their environment in a totally passive manner as they leave all domestic issues to the Agency. Integration of the complex with the surrounding urban centre of Bollate is extremely difficult. The place is hardly safe, with many open-air means of access, and its open-air ground floor is a vast abandoned space filled with rubbish.

The self-organized Korean settlements, however, seem to have withstood the test of time far better than their institutional competitor, the award-winning Social Housing Project. As a matter of fact, the Bollate Municipality had to invest a huge amount of resources to revitalize the Project just three decades after its construction, while the Koreas have been self-sustaining. Under pressure from inhabitants, which was manifested by a long local process, the municipality decided to elect for complete demolition and rebuilding. However, the architect himself opposed to this idea, and he applied to the National Authority for Built Heritage, claiming that his masterpiece be formally listed as piece of art. He succeeded. This prevented the demolition and a new restoration of the complex was proposed. As a result, nothing has happened thus far, and the Project remains in a horrendous state and a threat to its inhabitants.

This case illustrates the fact that upgraded informal settlements can sometimes provide a better housing solution than massive social housing projects.

Streets of Bollate

B. Illegal subdivisions

Some of the informal settlements in the region are not necessarily poor quality, under serviced housing areas. Residents in these settlements often have a title to the land, but the housing is built without a planning and/or building permit. Unauthorized land developments or illegal subdivisions are widespread on the fringes of cities in South-Eastern Europe—from Serbia to Bosnia and Herzegovina and Greece. Illegal subdivisions refer to settlements where agricultural land has been subdivided and sold by its legal owner to people who build their houses, often with self-help methods. Peri-urban land is transformed to urban use by landowners without any official planning permission and licenses. In some countries, the process has been commodified and used by developers to provide housing to middle-class families (e.g. in Italy and Turkey). The example in box 3 illustrates this process in Naples. The settlements are illegal because they might violate land-use planning, the standard of infrastructure is low and the land subdivision often does not meet planning standards for right-of-way, road access and provision of public space. Nevertheless, the housing built, while often constructed with permanent materials, may not meet building standards. In practice, these settlements are often tolerated due to populist politics and legalized though incorporation in the city's urban plan over time. It is important to mention that mass legalization has never been applied in Greece without an urban regeneration programme. Legalization has occurred only after the integration into the city plan and only after the completion of the necessary environmental improvements and infrastructure provisions, and most importantly, only after an individual inspection of the soundness of each construction and examination of its environmental impact. This is the major difference between the approaches used in Albania, Italy and Turkey and the Greek approach.

Most occupants of illegal subdivisions build, extend and improve their own housing over time. In practice, not all dwellings in such settlements are owner-occupied; they tend to be part of a vibrant rental housing market, controlled by individual homeowners and by speculative developers. Private-sector (developers') involvement must be formalized.

Similar examples of illegal subdivisions across the region are associated with extra-urban settlements in recreation zones and coastal areas. The problem seems to appear in Albania, Croatia, Cyprus Greece, Italy and Spain, where such responses may be driven by profit and speculative investment in a growing market for vacation homes, but also first residences in a better environment. These may be low-density housing developments in rural areas, with construction of good quality.

It is worth mentioning here the innovative approach applied in the municipality of Keratea (not a wealthy area), in Greece (Potsiou and Dimitriadi 2008), where the regeneration and expansion of city plans and the provision of the necessary improvements are all fully funded by the owners. This fact proves that people in general, even if not rich, are willing to pay in order to legalize their status and improve their neighborhoods. Often it is unrealistic procedures and long delays that invite an illegal approach.

Box 3: Illegal subdivisions in Naples, Italy

Illegally constructed neighborhoods in Naples house middle-class families. The best known case is Pianura, a neighbourhood that sprung up during the 1980s, when five- to seven-storey buildings were built without authorization from the city in an area classified as agricultural. The development is illegal in the technical sense of having no building permits and violating the zoning plan; but the land was legally bought by private developers who built the housing in compliance with existing building standards. The housing was sold at prices only 15–20 per cent below the cost of legal units. With the connivance of the authorities, the development was linked to the public water and electricity system, and later to the sewerage system. Growth in Pianura is still strong – increasing from 38,500 residents in 1981 to 54,000 in 1991, with higher homeownership rates than the city average. This type of illegal construction is widespread outside of the centre of Naples, leading to the emergence of many residential areas of different scale.

Source: *UN-HABITAT, 2003: 84.*

Figure 1: Typology of upgraded settlements and illegal suburban land subdivisions

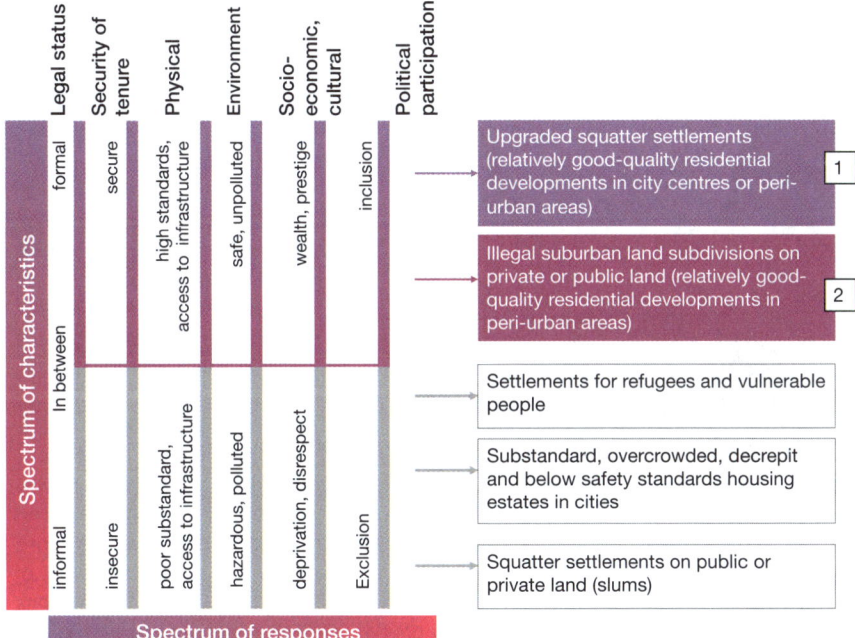

C. Settlements for vulnerable groups

Recently developed informal settlements by refugees and internally displaced persons (IDPs) across the UNECE region are often similar to the squatter type, but they might have been established with the permission of the State or the municipality as a temporary, rapid response to a major crisis, such as the war-related conflicts in Armenia, Azerbaijan, Cyprus and the Balkans. These settlements, although newer, often present extremely poor living conditions. Often, residents expected to stay only a short time, but the solution turned out to be more permanent, attracting more people to the original group. These temporary settlements are generally found in the urban periphery, in pockets of marginal land or close to collective centres for refugees.

Similarly to Azerbaijan (box 4), informal settlements for refugees, IDPs and victims of earthquakes, providing basic shelter in overcrowded slum type conditions, exist in Cyprus, Montenegro, Turkey and the Caucasus. In Armenia, about 40,000 families are without permanent shelter, mostly refugees or victims of the 1988 earthquake. About 40 per cent of these live in temporary structures, domiki ("little houses") or small caravans set up in public places. Dormitories and damaged unsafe housing provide shelter to another 10 per cent. Others live in former hotels, schools and kindergartens converted to temporary housing, which is also the case in Georgia. These vulnerable groups continue to face poor housing conditions and significant obstacles both to return and local integration (IDMC 2007).

Box 4: The housing crisis of refugees and displaced people in Azerbaijan

There are currently close to 1 million refugees and IDPs in Azerbaijan. This makes up 12 per cent of the total population. Although 14 years have passed since the beginning of Armenia-Azerbaijan conflict, over 1,722 refugee households have not been permanently settled. Within the IDP population, there is still a sizeable group living in unsatisfactory and precarious conditions. After 10 years, over 55,000 still live in tent camps, 32,000 in prefabricated temporary houses, 57,000 in farms and dugouts, 8,000 in railway cars and the rest in hostels, public buildings and unfinished construction buildings with no utilities. Long-term solutions are being envisaged through resettlement (as the new homes in Walicki demonstrate) or restitution and compensation schemes. The Government of Azerbaijan has allocated some 60,000 ha of State and municipal land to IDPs, and has created 760 farms providing livelihoods for about 47,000 IDPs so far.

Source: *Ministry of Economy of Azerbaijan, 2003.*

Figure 2: Substandard inner-city housing and settlements for vulnerable groups

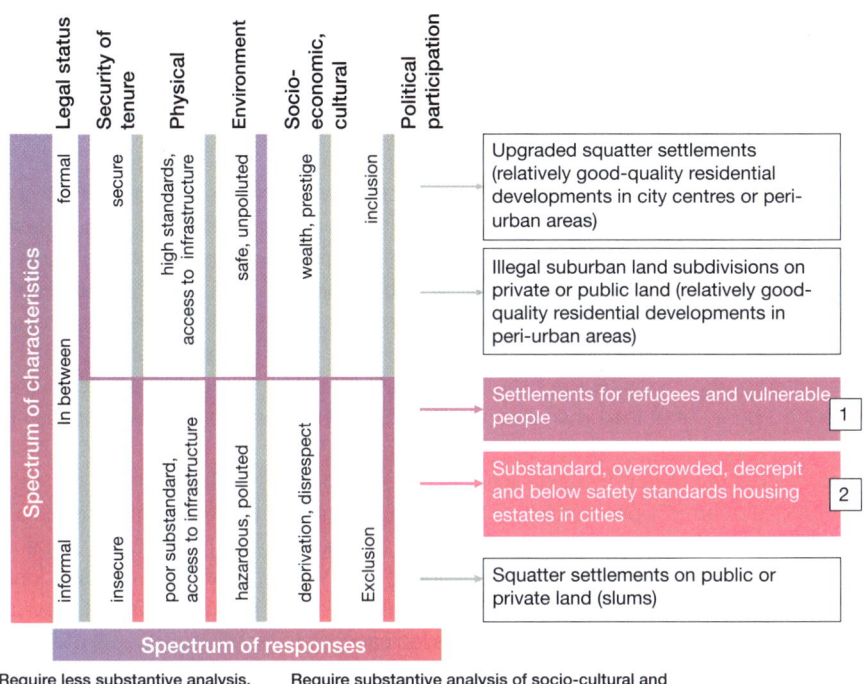

Require less substantive analysis, address visible characteristics

Require substantive analysis of socio-cultural and political problematic of IS residence

D. Substandard inner-city housing

Overcrowded, dilapidated housing without adequate facilities in city centres or densely urbanized areas is a form of informal settlement that is widely spread across the region. These inner-city neighborhoods with slum-like conditions originally developed as planned areas. They gradually have lost their attractiveness over time and have become home to low-income residents and illegal migrants living in overcrowded and substandard conditions. The systematic lack of investment to maintain the buildings in the areas has gradually eroded their quality over time. Although initially well serviced by infrastructure, further subdivisions of apartments, shared facilities and obsolete technical systems may have contributed to the premature aging of the housing stock. Examples include public housing projects, but more often private rental housing for industry workers and single-room-occupancy hotels. In general, occupants pay controlled rent and value the units' inner-city location, which gives them easy access to casual jobs and services.

Security of tenure in these types of informal settlements might not be a problem, but the quality of housing is a major concern. Substandard housing is defined as housing with at least one of the following problems: (a) housing built for temporary use; (b) housing units not fulfilling the minimal regulatory requirements specified in building codes; (c) housing without basic utility services (indoor toilets and bathrooms); or (d) housing in structurally unsound buildings with bad physical conditions. There is no systematic data across countries on these conditions, making comparisons particularly difficult.

In Western Europe, for example, the proportion of people facing at least one problem (e.g. overcrowding, inadequate living conditions related to dampness, darkness of housing, lack of ventilation or lack of indoor facilities) shows that several countries tend to have a higher share of people living in this type of substandard housing (close to 25 per cent – examples can be found in Belgium, France Luxembourg and Spain). In Portugal, this share is as high as 40 per cent (Eurostat 2007). Among the transition countries, some estimates by UN-HABITAT and UNECE indicate that about 10 per cent of the urban population lives in slum conditions without access to basic services and/or in overcrowded dwellings (UNECE 2004). In Central Asia, more than half of the urban population lives in slums (56 per cent in Tajikistan, 52 per cent in Kyrgyzstan and 51 per cent in Uzbekistan). Elsewhere in the region, these rates are 30 per cent for Kazakhstan and the Republic of Moldova and 19 per cent in Bosnia and Herzegovina, Croatia, Romania and the former Yugoslav Republic of Macedonia (UN-HABITAT 2005a). Although urban areas reportedly have higher levels of service, close to 3 million people in European cities lack access to piped water and 8 million to sewerage (UN-HABITAT 2005a).

Countries in transition have a significant share of their housing stock poorly serviced by piped water and sewers. Data indicate that the situation regarding piped water supply in the housing stock in the EECCA[4] countries is particularly problematic in Republic of Moldova and Uzbekistan, with services available in one third of the stock. In Eastern and South-Eastern Europe, Albania and Romania stand out with half of the housing lacking piped water. As in the case of water supply, sewerage services are most problematic in Albania, Romania and the EECCA countries. The data indicate that a limited share of the housing has a bath or shower—Uzbekistan (13.3 per cent), Bosnia and Herzegovina (22 per cent), Kyrgyzstan (24 per cent) and the Republic of Moldova and Turkmenistan (30 per cent).

In addition, the share of substandard housing has increased dramatically in war affected countries. In Bosnia and Herzegovina, these challenges are particularly significant. Some 445,000 homes in the country have been partially or totally destroyed, which is more than a 37 per cent of pre-war housing stock. In Kosovo (Serbia), 30 per cent of the housing stock was damaged, while in Croatia the damaged and

---

[4] Eastern Europe, Caucasus and Central Asia. The EECCA countries are Armenia, Azerbaijan, Belarus, Georgia, Kazakhstan, Kyrgyzstan, Republic of Moldova, Russian Federation, Tajikistan, Turkmenistan, Ukraine and Uzbekistan..

demolished housing stock is over 200.000 dwelling units, or close to 13 per cent of the country total (Wegelin 2003).

E.   Squatter settlements

One of the most enduring manifestations of informal settlements, and one that has attracted the most attention, is squatter housing. Squatter settlements are settlements established by people who have illegally occupied an area of land and built their houses on it, usually through self-help processes. Terms associated with this type of spontaneous settlement in the UNECE region are shanty towns, peri-urban settlements and slums. Terms in other languages include *baracas, favelas, bidonvilles, gecekondu, chabolas* and *novostroiki.*

Squatter settlements are part of the urban landscape in more than 15 countries in the region. Some, in Southern Europe date back to the 1960s; others in the post-socialist countries of former Yugoslavia were established in the 1970s and 1980s, while in Central Asia they have a much more recent origin – the early 1990s. These settlements are primarily the result of rapid influxes to cities due to migration and changes in the urban economies, or as a result of a gradual process of occupation and incremental growth. The settlements, often in peri-urban areas and on public or private land, have grown to become municipalities in their own right, housing hundreds of thousands of people. Over time, housing has been followed by some ad hoc development of small-scale retail and services in response to local demand. These are indeed signals of a spontaneous evolution towards more complex and organized settlements, which must be supported. Such community processes may be valuable resources, contributing to better policy outcomes.

Although the initial settlements may have been the result of the authorities turning a blind eye, particularly during the immediate post-socialist inflow of migrants to the cities, today the scale of these developments presents a severe problem. For example, in Albania informal settlements contain up to a quarter of the population in major cities and account for 40 per cent of the built-up area (box 5). In the former Yugoslav Republic of Macedonia, they are home to 11 per cent of the population in the 14 largest cities. In Belgrade, informal settlements take up to 40 per cent of the residential areas. In Kyrgyzstan, 150,000 to 200,000 people have migrated to Bishkek from the provinces in the past five years. Osh, the country's second largest city, has seen a similar influx, resulting in informal substandard housing on the outskirts. The housing units often lack basic necessities such as sanitation and running water (IFC 2006).

In addition to the large peri-urban squatter settlements, there are many other examples of smaller pockets of informal housing built illegally under bridges and overpasses and on vacant plots of land close to industrial zones and railway reserves, river banks, landslides, waste dumps and landfill sites. The land, which may be public

Box 5: Informal settlements in Tirana

The estimated population of the Tirana region grew from 374,000 in 1990 to 618,000 in 1999. Close to 55 per cent of the population lives in informal settlements. Incoming villagers occupy a plot of land and start building a house, adding floors and finishing construction over time. As a result, Bathore, an attractive hillside on the outskirts of Tirana, is a new neighbourhood of illegal three-storey houses with no roads, sewerage or electricity. Those who first occupy the land then illegally sell parts to newcomers. Illegal construction usually means no access to schools or health care.

Source: UNECE 2002.

Box 6: Housing exclusion: the case of Roma communities

The Roma in Serbia and Montenegro often live in unsafe and impoverished areas. They build housing by themselves using non-durable materials or employing unused old railway cars, buses, etc. The majority of their housing units are, in fact huts, shacks or so-called tent settlements. In a number of these settlements, connections to water tend to be illegal; there is no waste collection, no sewerage systems and no indoor plumbing. In Serbia, arout 70 per cent of Roma households reportedly live in dwellings with no water connection, over 80 per cent with no sewerage and 65 per cent in illegally built settlements. In Montenegro, 32 per cent of the Roma live in collective centres and 47.6 per cent in barracks, while 45 per cent lack plumbing and tap water at home.

Source: World Bank, 2005.

or private, is unstable or unsuitable for urban development, of less value, and has no services and access to essential infrastructure. These marginal squatter settlements are often makeshift, built with temporary materials, and the residents often face a threat of eviction and demolition. The location and conditions in these squatter settlements are immensely diverse, but more importantly, their residents often face multiple exclusion. Roma communities, mahalas dating back to the nineteenth century, are unfortunate examples of this situation.[5] The evidence below highlights the dimensions of the problems in marginalized squatter settlements in many cities in the region (box 6).

Figure 3: Typology of squatter settlements

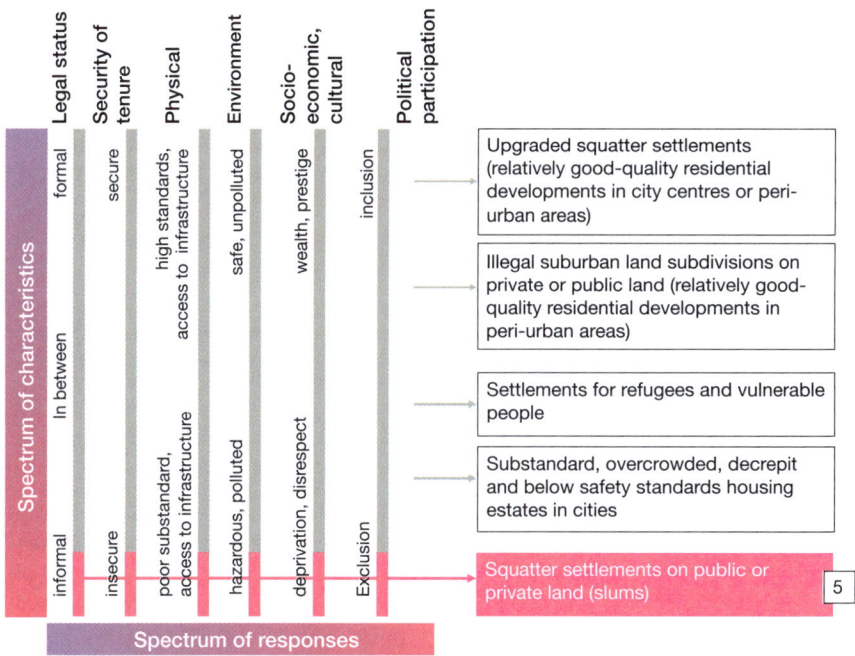

Require less substantive analysis, address visible characteristics

Require substantive analysis of socio-cultural and political problematic of IS residence

---

[5] Romania has the highest absolute number of Roma in Europe – between 1 and 2 million – with these numbers somewhat lower in Bulgaria, Hungary and Slovakia. In other parts of Europe, the largest Roma populations live in Spain (about 600,000), France (about 300,000), Germany (about 70,000) and Italy (about 100,000).

Box 7: City profile: Bishkek

The development of informal settlements in Bishkek took place during two periods, the first from 1990 to 1993, when the Kyrgyz Republic became independent, and the second after 2005 during the political turbulence in the country.

During these two periods, internal migration was high, especially from south to north Kyrgyzstan, and led to an unbalanced and rapid growth of urban population. Data from National Statistical Committee of Kyrgyz Republic indicate that the population in Bishkek increased from 619,903 to 841,800 between 1989 and 2008. Overpopulation, a growing demand for housing and the lack of social housing have consequently caused the formation of informal settlements around the city. Informal settlements in Bishkek are called *novostroiki* ("new settlements"). Nowadays, the term is used to indicate the areas where people have illegally occupied the land to build their own houses.

Between 1990 and 1993, the first wave of immigrants occupied the agricultural land around the city, resulting in the creation of 27 *novostroiki*. Citizens, according to the Land Code, are to be allocated land plots (300 or 400 m^2) free-of-charge: (a) for the construction of a residential house; (b) for the construction of a dacha (summer house); and (c) for agricultural land use for the entitled citizens.

During the second wave of migration, which started in 2005, many people came to Bishkek to protest after the revolution, and they started to illegally occupy the land.

Many *novostroiki* in area surrounding Bishkek have no access to safe water; only between 10 and 50 per cent of households have regular access to piped water, and of those, only one quarter has in-house connections, with the remainder using yard standpipes. According to a World Bank report, public standpipes, water from trucks, and sewage systems do not exist, and nearly all *novostroiki* residents use pit latrines. Waste collection is poor: most *novostroiki* are not served by the city trash collection services, although some have been reported to organize their own occasional pick-up campaigns. Access to social services remains limited. The provision of basic infrastructure, of crucial importance, should be the responsibility of local government, but so far limited financial and human resources have prevented them from improving the situation.

In addition, the fact that settlements are randomly organized and located on agricultural land outside the city centre adds to the difficulties of providing basic infrastructure and of including the settlements into the economical and social life of Bishkek.

The problems of those settlements are further complicated by the inadequate depth of the foundation of the single-floor, brick construction which provokes dilatation and restriction under the building, with related breakages of walls. In addition, the general lack of adequate thermal performance and the cool air inhaled during the wintertime result in lung diseases such as tuberculosis, which are common among settlers. Medical care is only available in some of the *novostroiki*.

The majority of the second wave of migrants living in *novostroiki* arrived from rural areas. Most were herders. While their cultural heritage could ensure a better quality and safety for the houses (while herders, they formerly lived mainly in yurts, which are both soundly constructed and sustainable), but uncertainty about the legal status of landownership and occupancy rights has led to provisional ways of building. Indeed, while waiting for government intervention, most have opted for provisional rather than safe housing, which in the long term squanders the indigenous know-how and traditions with respect to construction.

Today, Bishkek has about 50 such settlements with a population of – depending on the estimates – between 125,000 and 200,000. In 2005, the World Bank estimated that in Bishkek only 15 per cent of adults in *novostroiki* had formal and permanent employment, and about 30 per cent worked in the informal sector.

Social tensions in the *novostroiki* are common and regularly lead to riots and protests. Nevertheless, the social and family structures offer some social security, and should be considered as precious social capital.

The solution to the critical situation of the *novostroiki* is provided mainly by the Government's allocation of land plots to the occupants and the provision of basic infrastructure. However, this is a lengthy process, and despite the existence of the Land Code, the second wave of migrants still lives in an illegal situation years after their arrival.

3. Location and size

Informal settlements tend to cluster in two very broad types of locations: inner-city areas and peri-urban areas. The centrality of location often implies older, more established formations close to the old city or its industrial zones. Residents benefit from the proximity of employment opportunities, but often inhabit substandard housing on sites that are exposed to environmental and health risks, and are normally unfit for urban development. In most cases, informal settlements – especially large-scale formations – concentrate in the periphery (because of limited land supply and a lack of housing programmes for low-income groups or a lack of spatial planning and instruments to integrate low-income groups into wider socio-economic processes at different spatial levels). These could be squatter settlements on public land or illegal subdivisions outside urban/municipal boundaries. The quality and standards of housing are generally better, and some illegal connections to existing infrastructure may ensure much-needed electricity and water. Residents of these settlements are relatively effective in resisting attempts to demolish or relocate them. In some cases (for instance, Romania), due to active leadership, residents negotiate inclusion in the urban boundaries relatively quickly – particularly if the land is legally owned – and then leverage investment in roads and infrastructure.

Although some of these settlements have been upgraded over time, urban problems are manifested in inadequate infrastructure, water and electricity shortages and limited access to services such as education and health (UN-HABITAT 2002a). The legalization of these settlements requires significant investment. Necessary investment may be funded by the penalties applied to the legalization of the informal buildings and by the regular revenue from real estate taxation, which must be reinvested in the neighborhoods. A study of how similar investments are made in Europe to urbanize rural land in countries with less flexible planning systems has shown that landowners must contribute with both land and money. In Germany, owners contribute with land and in addition pay 90 per cent of the costs for the necessary infrastructure to integrate areas into the city plan. In Greece, where most areas under urbanization include informal settlements, owners pay a lower percentage of the costs for infrastructure improvements and additional founds are provided by the State (with some exceptions, e.g. the municipality of Keratea). Owners, however, always must contribute a much more significant portion of their parcels in order to provide the necessary land for roads, parking, squares and parks, sports facilities, hospitals, schools and churches, etc. (Potsiou and Mueller 2007).

Table 2: Matrix of informal settlement types

	Inner-city	Peri-urban	Substandard/Slums	Relatively good quality
Squatter settlements on public or private land	●	●	●	
Settlements for refugees and vulnerable people	●		●	
Upgraded squatter settlements	●	●		●
Illegal suburban land subdivisions on private or public land		●		●
Overcrowded, dilapidated housing without adequate facilities	●		●	

4. Factors influencing the development of informal settlements

Countries in the UNECE region have a range of housing and land provision systems. They also have different planning and cadastral systems (Enemark 2007), and in general different approaches to land development and land-related public administration structures. This legacy is an important determinant of housing conditions and persisting problems with informal settlements. The problem is significant in a little

Box 8: The slumification of housing in Russian cities

Housing stock

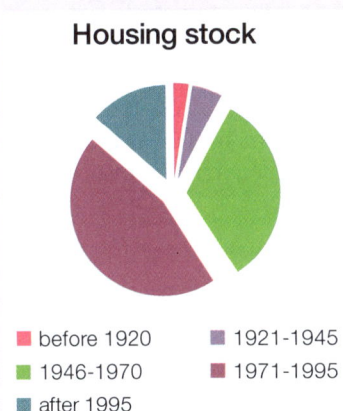

- before 1920
- 1921-1945
- 1946-1970
- 1971-1995
- after 1995

Since 2007, the Russian Federation has been fighting a growing degeneration of multi-family housing. At that time, then-President Vladimir Putin identified this as "a national shame".

A large share of the Russian housing stock was the result of a major construction boom initiated by Khrushchev in 1951. In the context of acute housing shortages and low living standards, Khrushchev managed to provide the majority of Russian citizens with decent housing. This housing was planned. however, to have a 25-year or 50-year lifespan. Due to chronic under-repair during the Soviet period and further negligence after 1991, Russian housing stock degraded considerably. Moreover, Soviet-era housing stock does not meet contemporary living standards and nor does it fit into the new urban structures of the new market economy.

Today, 78 per cent of the overall housing stock is privately owned and 20 per cent State/municipal property. State/municipal housing accommodates urban tenants and it is predominantly this housing that is in the worst condition.

Residents in multi-family housing have in reality received only partial control of the multi-family buildings (mainly control over their apartments), as in many cases the authorities maintain control over the land and communal areas. A major implication is uncertainty over who should take care of these communal areas, and has led to increased degradation of privatized housing stock. On the other hand, tenants in non-privatized municipal housing are trapped in worse living conditions and lack good access to utilities. It is argued that such housing is undergoing still more rapid degradation.

According to 2007 estimates, about 40 per cent of the Russian housing stock required major housing revamping, with a cost of 1.3 trillion roubles. At the time, in many regions of the Russian Federation the share of degraded multi-family housing was 17–25 per cent. According to government statistical data, in 2008 registered degraded and unsafe housing reached 98 million m^2, or 3.2 per cent of the overall housing stock.

less than half of the UNECE Member States (20 countries) and affects the lives of over 50 million people. The critical factors affecting the formation of informal settlements are notably related to several major interrelated changes, inter alia: (a) rapid urbanization and influx of people into select urban areas; (b) war and natural disasters leading to massive movement of people to places of opportunity and safety; (c) poverty and the lack of low-cost housing and serviced land; and (d) inefficient public administration, inappropriate planning and inadequate land administration tools.

Manifestations of informality are attributed to the lack of effective planning, effective land administration systems and spatial planning for urban and rural development. Institutional constraints, coupled with a legacy of ineffective policies dealing with the problem of illegal construction on a large scale, often perpetuate this cycle of informality. While large-scale peri-urban informal settlements are an integral part of the urban landscape in just less than half of the UNECE region, overcrowded, dilapidated housing without adequate facilities in city centres or densely urbanized areas – another slum type of informal settlement formation – is a problem in all 56 UNECE member States. It is therefore necessary that problems contributing to the formation of these

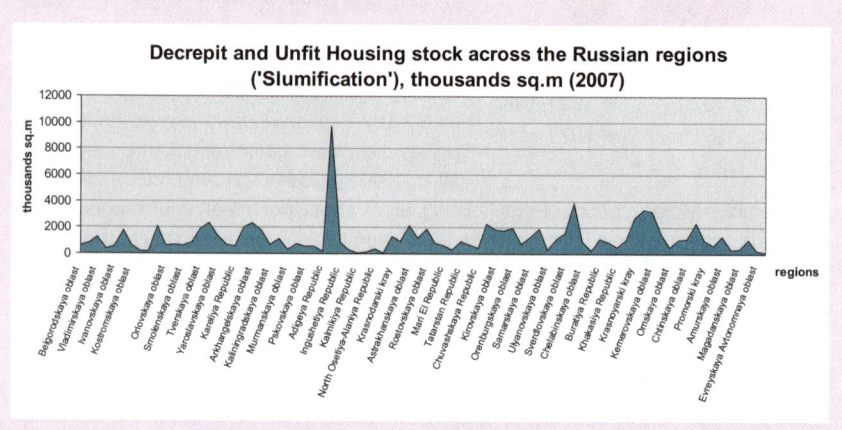

In July 2007, the Law on the Foundation for Assistance in the Reformation of Housing and Utility Sector was approved, and in November 2007 the State-run "Foundation for Assistance in the Reformation of Housing and Utility Sector" was established. The latter was designated to allocate 240 billion roubles among the country's regions. The Foundation pursues two major objectives: the creation of "responsible citizens" and the elimination of unfit housing and utility infrastructure. Funding limits for each of the regions are defined by the following formula: 240 billion roubles multiplied by the share of the region's housing stock of the Russian Federation's total housing stock. Furthermore, the fund of 240 billion roubles is to be distributed in the following proportions: 60 per cent for major repairs of decrepit housing and 40 per cent for resettlement and elimination of unfit housing.

different types of informal settlements are properly acknowledged and appropriate policies designed.

Notwithstanding these differences, housing policy and land management responses to the challenges of informal settlements in the last decade need to be reviewed in the context of economic, social and urban change. These drivers in different countries increasingly map a diverse set of policy challenges, and correspondingly, a very diverse set of approaches. The following sections will focus on some of the major aspects of change influencing the political economic and social context in which informal settlements develop, as well as underlying policy interventions.

Uneven redistribution of the fund

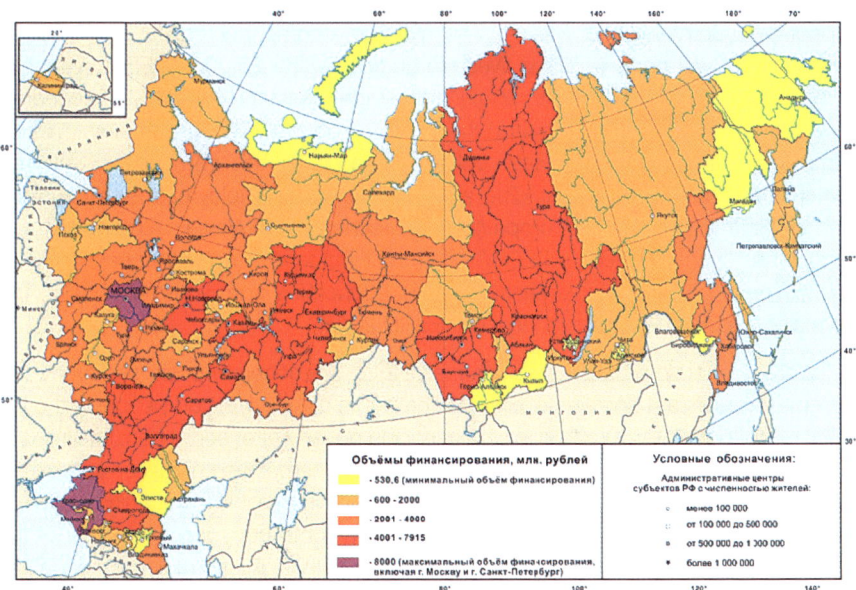

A. Economic and social change

The problem of informal settlements in its most acute manifestation is found mostly in low-income countries in the UNECE region. It is directly related to weak land administration and lack of security of land tenure. Lower levels of economic and social development, coupled with significant economic restructuring in the last decade, were a major driver of dislocations and adjustment in the economies of cities and rural communities. Rising unemployment, poverty and instability also acted as drivers of rapid migration to places with jobs. Incidentally, these countries also have lower level of urbanization. These relationships are not necessarily straightforward, but need to be understood in the context of economic and social change affecting the countries' growth trajectories.

Nevertheless, most countries across the region have experienced economic growth in the last decade, with high gross domestic product (GDP) growth rates in transition countries following prolonged recessions. Despite the uneven performance, this has delivered better living standards in Western Europe, North America and some of the Central European countries. Some of the major economic and social indicators that characterize the diverse performance in the 56 countries in the UNECE region are presented in annex 1.

The recent expansion of the EU, with 10 more Member States joining in 2005 and another two in 2007, has provided a major boost for better economic performance in the newest Member States. Macroeconomic data indicate that growth prospects in the euro zone are modest, with the loss of momentum more apparent in the biggest economies, Germany and France. The average income per capita, measured in purchasing power parity (PPP), in Western Europe is US$ 25,000; in EECCA it tends to be as low as $2,500 (UNECE, 2007). This crude measure of the level of economic development divides the countries in the region up into very different clusters, making generalizations about appropriate policies to address the challenge of informal settlements particularly difficult. The average level of unemployment has remained high in Central and Eastern Europe (26.7 per cent) and in Western Europe (7.6 per cent), while unemployment in EECAA has remained as low as 2.5 per cent (UNECE 2007). These countries have sheltered their economies from external shocks, but have also experienced deep recessions (EBRD 2006).

While economic prospects across the UNECE are generally positive, poverty has become a significant social and political challenge. Over 74 million people in the EU live in risk of poverty, with one in six experiencing poverty after social transfers in 2005 (Eurostat 2007). Groups at risk are the long-term unemployed, large or one-parent families, people with low levels of education and – increasingly – ethnic minorities, with particularly deep pockets of poverty among Roma communities. Some of the common drivers are unemployment or jobless growth, but also regional inequalities and inadequacy of the social protection systems (European Commission 2004). By contrast, the dimensions of poverty in EECAA are quite different. The sub-region accounts for the largest share of people living in absolute poverty. While at the start of the reform, poverty in countries in transition did not exist in the present-day sense of the concept, today more than 100 million people are classified as poor (World Bank 2002). Percentages of people living on less than $1 per day are alarmingly high in Armenia (12 per cent), Tajikistan (12 per cent) and Uzbekistan (19 per cent). Appropriate general legislative and administrative reforms are still needed, including those related to land and real estate property.

Within the context of rapid economic and social change in at least half of the countries in the UNECE region, the growth of informal settlements is perhaps less surprising. Growing affordability problems – particularly in low income countries, where the combination of high unemployment, poverty and social polarization adversely affect people's ability to house themselves – is part of the informal settlements challenge. Furthermore, pressures to reduce government deficits and redirect spending priorities towards more productive sectors of the economy also reduce the abilities of countries to comprehensively addressing informal settlements. In several countries within or outside the European region with free–market economies, the informal housing sector has become practically a part of housing sector – or an alternative, within a free market economy, to the lack of affordable State-owned housing (Potsiou 2007). Given that the majority of existing informal construction is of relatively good quality and cannot be characterized as slums, the informal housing sector has been "quietly" supported by certain Governments, and is now acquiring growing recognition. The old theory, which viewed informal settlements as "threats to public safety and health requiring demolition", seems to have been gradually replaced by a common recognition that informal housing is a valuable capital asset that should find its way to the real property market (De Soto 2000).

B. Urban change: urbanization and migration

The UNECE region is highly urbanized, with more than 75 per cent of the population concentrated in urban areas, and is facing a growing complexity of urban challenges. The level of urbanization in Western Europe is 80 per cent, with that in the United Kingdom and Belgium exceeding 90 per cent. In North America, over 80 per cent of the population is urbanized. Countries in transition, e.g. the Russian Federation (73.3 per cent), Poland (62 per cent), the Czech Republic (74.5 per cent) and Hungary (65.9 per cent), have an average rate of urbanization close to 61 per cent, which is considerably higher in the largest countries. These patterns are presented in figure 4.

With the exception of seven mega-cities – Chicago, Istanbul, London, Los Angeles, Moscow, New York and Paris – most cities in the region tend to be under 3 million with medium densities, stable or low-growth populations and growth rates of under 1 per cent. Close to 45 per cent of the population of the UNECE region lives in medium-sized cities with a population of 100,000 to 200,000. The region has 100 cities with population of over 1 million (UN-HABITAT 2005a). Annual urban growth rates in Italy, Portugal and Turkey are comparable to those in the United States and Canada, and tend to gravitate around 1.1–1.4 per cent.

In less urbanized countries (e.g. Albania, Azerbaijan, Tajikistan and Uzbekistan), the projected annual urban growth exceeds 2 per cent (see annex 1). What is more important is that this growth is spatially concentrated in several cities, often the national capitals, resulting in disproportionate increases in population over a very short period of time. While certain cities have exploded in the early 1990s, the rest of the country might experience negative population growth – a result of emigration, lower reproduction rates and responses to economic hardship. For example, population growth from 1998 to 2005 in Tajikistan was 16.5 per cent, and was mostly channelled to Dushanbe, the capital. The city's population is now close to 1 million, creating a potential deficit of 100,000 dwellings. Similarly, in Kyrgyzstan the population has grown from 4.7 million in 1997 to 5.1 million in 2005. Bishkek, with 200,000 migrants from rural areas, reportedly experiences acute housing shortages, with the result of peri-urban expansion of informal settlements (IFC 2006).

These high levels of urbanization create significant challenges for the provision of affordable and adequate housing in large cities. Despite the notable economic success of major urban centres in the UNECE region today, globalization has exacerbated social polarization and urban poverty. In countries in transition, the change from centrally planned economies to market-based one has added further layers of complexity. In many of these countries, a decline in living conditions has been accompanied by the rapid deterioration of existing housing, homelessness and the formation of informal settlements (UN-HABITAT 2005a, 2007). The urban poor living in these settlements are especially vulnerable both politically and economically: they lack access to services, safety nets and political representation. Cumulative disadvantages – often defined along the lines of gender, age and ethnicity – create widening social divides between social groups, with low-income, single-parent or women-led households being the worst off.

Figure 4: Urbanization in the UNECE region, 2005

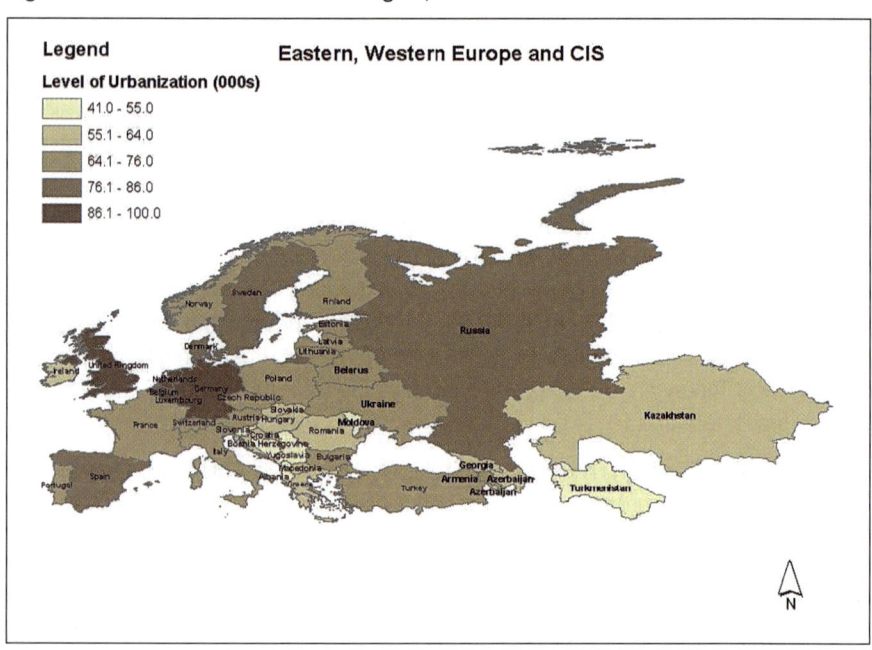

Source: Based on Data from UN-HABITAT, 2007

C. The crisis of displaced people and refugees

In addition to the challenges associated with urbanization and poverty, many countries in the UNECE region are or have been affected by war or civil conflicts. Almost 7 million have become refugees or IDPs in the last decade. Military conflicts and violence in the Balkans and Northern Caucasus and Armenia has caused long-term stress on the housing systems of these countries. Across the region, internal displacement continues to be a major problem in the Balkans, the Caucasus, Turkey and Cyprus, reaching a total number of IDPs 2.8 million in the region(table 3). South-Eastern Europe has experienced the largest refugee crisis in Europe since the Second World War. By 1995, the region witnessed the displacement of more than 2 million people, making for unique housing challenges. Serbia and Montenegro still host the largest number of refuges and IDPs in Europe, including 226,106 IDPs from Kosovo (Serbia). Refugees and IDPs are often the residents of informal settlements, although in some cases families remain in collective centres and refugee camps. Creating an atmosphere for sustainable return through the effective implementation of the rights to property, education, housing, health care and employment should be an integral part of the overall strategy in countries affected by the refugee and IDP crisis (IDMC, 2007; Wegelin, 2003).

Several countries in Europe and North America have become the home of a significant number of refugees and asylum-seekers. The data in table 3 presents the number of refugees in countries where pressures are significant. Geopolitical changes of the past decade, in particular the liberalization of movements of persons from Central and Eastern Europe, have enlarged the geographical frame of reference for international migration. The growth of migration flows originating from Romania, Ukraine and war-torn countries in the Balkans to Germany, United Kingdom and Switzerland – and more recently, Italy and the Scandinavian countries – has increased significantly. Immigrants often settle in the capital cities, and in some cases become part of the underground economy.[6]

The integration of immigrants remains a major issue for many countries in the UNECE region, particularly those with limited ability to provide adequate shelter and social assistance. Most countries increasingly rely on a mix of integration and assimilation policies promoting market-based solutions to housing choices (CECODHAS 2007). In certain countries (e.g. Canada, Greece, Italy and the United States), the lack of policies aimed at improving housing for refugees and immigrants in the context of an exclusively private housing provision has resulted in growing housing problems and squatting. For example, in Italy the housing problems of immigrants

---

[6] The overwhelming majority of migrants enter South European countries without a residence permit, which they obtain thanks to frequent legalization schemes. (Since 1986, there have been five in Italy, four in Spain, three in Portugal, one in Greece.) Taking into account all the applications filed for legalization, one can estimate that three out of four people in Italy, more than half in Spain, over 30 per cent in Portugal, and 9 out of 10 in Greece are unauthorized (Jahn and Straubhaar 1999).

have been defined as "dramatic" (Mandic 2006), particularly the undocumented or "irregular" immigrants living in slums and squatter settlements. In Greece, only half of the country's 1 million immigrants are recorded and the situation in reception centres for refugees is reportedly inadequate (ibid., 2006).

Table 3: Refugees and displaced persons in the UNECE region

Country	Refugees	Displaced persons
Azerbaijan		686, 586
Bosnia and Herzegovina	22,223	186,451
Cyprus		210,000
Georgia		247,000
Russian Federation	102,965	158,900
Serbia and Montenegro	149,915	226,106
Turkey		953,680–1,201,200
Canada	147,171	
France	137,316	
Germany	700,016	
Netherlands	118,189	
Switzerland	48,030	
United Kingdom	293,459	
United States	379,340	

Sources: Refugee data refer to UN-HABITAT 2005, 2007b; IDP data to IDMC 2007.

Box 9: City profile: Prijedor, Bosnia and Herzegovina

The municipality of Prijedor, located in the north-western part of Bosnia and Herzegovina, is one of the cities that suffered the most from the violence and atrocities of the war. During the period 1992–1995 more than 50 per cent of the 112,543 inhabitants (1991 population census) emigrated from the region.

The 1995 internationally sponsored Dayton Agreement7 that ended the war in Bosnia also mandated extensive property restitution to encourage the refugees' return. A decade after these provisions were implemented, the Bosnian experience is recognized as an important learning experience in terms of the efficiency of the refugees property restitution process (Williams, 2007).

---

[7] General Framework Agreement for Peace in Bosnia and Herzegovina.

In Prijedor, 1,000 displaced persons returned to their pre-war homes. While there are no precise statistical population data, it is estimated that there now are about 25,000 immigrants in Prijedor; of these, 17,000 are displaced persons from Bosnia and Herzegovina and 2,000 are refugees, mainly from Croatia.

In Prijedor today, even though 2,000 housing units to provide shelter for displaced people have been built and most of the returnees' destroyed homes have been rebuilt, provision of adequate housing for all the immigrants is still a problem.

The unbalanced ratio between housing demand and supply, the lack of an urban and land administration system due to a transitional political period and the continuous flow of people to Prijedor have provoked the growth of informal settlements. This seems the quickest and most affordable solution that most people have found.

During 1999, the Municipal Assembly of Prijedor adopted the project, "Prijedor 2000: Home for All People", to solve the housing problems of refugees and displaced persons. However, the project was mainly limited to the distribution of a plot of agricultural land to each displaced family. This allocation took place without any prior assessment of the land to be allocated or an allocation strategy, and to date, basic urban services as water or sewage system are still lacking.

Nova Orlovaca, in south Prijedor, is one of the informal settlements developed after this land distribution. In the four years following the first land distribution in 1999, Nova Orlovaca has expanded: 386 buildings were built in 1999, and according to the last field survey undertaken by the Demographic Research Centre, there are now 502 buildings. Although several of these are located in the land allocated by the Municipality, none have the permission for building.

The population of Nova Orlovaca is now approximately 2,100 people, spread over four villages; the majority of inhabitants are refugees and some are of returnees.

Living conditions in Nova Orlovaca remain difficult: basic services are lacking, and only few settlements have safe water-supply systems or sewerage. There are no proper roads and no power grid. The northern borders of the settlements experience frequent problems with flooding. The main building typology consists of two-storey family buildings made of brick and concrete, without thermal isolation.

There are no laws on legalization and integration of informal settlements in Bosnia and Herzegovina, but Act 155 of the Law on Spatial Planning stipulates that every municipality should adopt decisions regarding the legalization of informal settlements.

In response to this Act, in 2005 the Municipality of Prijedor decided to start a project to legalize all the buildings in Nova Orlovaca. A parceling plan was developed to include the settlements in the cadastre system and a project was initiated for a sewage system and safe water provision.

This legalization process has been slowed by a number of obstacles, including the unclear land ownership. In fact, the owners of the agricultural land are taking legal action against the Municipality, which allowed the refugees to reoccupy their own land after the war.

Despite legal constraints, the Municipality is preparing a project for land drainage that will be implemented in 2009. A project for the sewage system for the entire area is ongoing and has been completed in a part of Nova Orlovaca.

In 2008, the Association of Town and Municipalities of Republic of Srpska, in collaboration with the Network of Association of Local Authorities for South-East Europe and with the support of GTZ8, initiated the "Urban Integration of Inform Settlements in the Municipality of Prijedor" project. Its goal is to monitor the planning process and to analyse legal frameworks that might have an effect on the preparation and implementation of the legalization process. A socio-economic study and detailed physical survey are being conducted to focus on the most affected areas and social strata.

Nova Orlovaca, in spite of its legal difficulties, is now undergoing a positive physical improvements thanks to the joint efforts of the municipality, residents and international organizations.

---

[8] German Agency for Economic Development.

CHAPTER 2

The Economic, Social and Environmental Challenges of Informal Settlements

Addressing the problems of informal settlements requires better understanding of the driving forces contributing to their expansion and growth. Countries in the region experiencing informal settlement growth are grappling with the same set of systemic problems related to lack of access to affordable housing, inappropriate spatial planning policies and an incomplete system of land management as well as growing urban poverty, though in very different national contexts. A common element of this process in transition countries is the combined effect of economic transformation and civil strife, which has provoked a sudden acceleration of urban migration and a proliferation of informal settlements in more than 12 countries. Central and local governments were largely unprepared to face the pressures on land, housing and services. Years after these conflicts, later illegal or informal construction covers large tracts of peri-urban land, and is home of both socially vulnerable groups and relatively well-off migrants to the cities.

As Gabriel (2007) states, "This is not simply an "urban planning problem", but a rather more complex and intractable phenomenon which, unless rapidly and efficiently addressed, may threaten the long-term sustainability of urban communities". Recognizing that the types and processes of informal settlement formation are multidimensional in nature, often varying widely between but mostly within the countries and cities, this section highlights the economic, social and environmental challenges associated with their proliferation.

1. The economic challenges

While research indicates that there is a growing acceptance of the "informal city" in most countries in the UNECE region, its economic, environmental and social challenges have largely been underestimated. The lack of affordable housing policies, the scale of the informal developments and their persistent presence in some cities has forced both international institutions and Governments to recognize the fact that informal settlements are here to stay. Interventions have moved towards the design of more efficient and practical ways to improve these neighborhoods through urban policies that are cost-effective and socially inclusive. Meanwhile, in the transition countries, the rapid growth of the "informal city" has been recognized as a manifestation of the largest economic challenge that local governments and cities must face.

In economic terms, informal settlements mobilize significant public and private investment that remains outside of the formal economy and investment cycles (De Soto 2003). In addition, they are associated with significant public-sector costs, both explicit and implicit. Settlements often take over public land, shifting the cost burden to local governments and public institutions. The land, often developed in a sporadic and expensive way with single-family housing, is underused due to its low density sprawling pattern. Informal settlements also impact on government's ability to manage and plan sustainable land use – as the owners illegally occupy park land and former industrial zones that are unsafe for residential development or occupy land that may have more productive commercial or social uses. While this might not be the highest and best use of the land, the squatting creates long-term problems for the orderly development and growth of the city as well as its servicing requirements and overall real estate potential. Owners usually do not pay property taxes or user fees; often they connect illegally to infrastructure, thus reducing the revenue available to government to provide essential services.

Informal settlements are a vital element of both the informal and formal economies and real estate market. Housing and land in these locations is traded without the involvement of real estate agencies, registration in the cadastre and required payments of State taxes and dues. While this makes housing more affordable and reduces transaction costs, it cannot be mortgaged or used as collateral for other business purposes (De Soto 2003).

At the same time, this might be a single largest asset of the residents in these peri-urban areas, and is boosted by sweat equity and remittances from family members. Since there is no tenure security in most cases, this investment is constantly under threat of being lost ("dead capital"), particularly due to environmental hazards (e.g. floods, landslides, earthquakes) or demolition in cases of road widening and other major infrastructure development. The informality of the market is not attractive to the owners, nor is it to the notaries, lawyers, surveyors, banks and insurance agencies involved. In the majority of cases, people and professionals are forced to become extralegal.

A number of remedies – ranging from the provision of basic services to social housing programmes and relocation – are regularly provided in order to open up formal markets to the marginalized groups in informal settlements. However, they have had a limited success. Informal practices remain the only affordable option for low-income groups to access housing and land. If informal settlement interventions are to be efficient and sustainable, the "achievements" and capacity of the informal sector to deliver assets to the poor must be appreciated.

Although there is still disagreement as to whether informality is part of the problem or a possible solution, informal strategies play an essential role in supporting the livelihood of a large part of the population in countries with informal settlements. While designing policy interventions, Governments must recognize this potential of the poor for self-provision and mutual support, as well that the informal sector helps the functioning of the urban economy. It is important to support such productive environments through integrating informal settlements with the formal economy. Creating opportunities for labour must be considered part of the solution to the problems of informal settlements. In the case of regeneration of neighborhoods, there are some good examples in international literature, e.g. in projects applied in several countries (including Austria, Germany and the United Kingdom), but also in Greece, India and elsewhere.

Notwithstanding the economic challenges for the individual residents, informal settlements pose a high political and economic cost for government, especially in cases of evictions, legalization and resettlement. Efforts to document the extent of informal development as well as to allocate the extra institutional capacity to integrate the settlements into the planned area of the city are extremely costly. Furthermore, local government and public institutions need to cope with land and real estate registration, dispute resolution, and in some cases compensation of private landowners. Often the inability to absorb these costs perpetuates tolerance of the "informal city".

2. The social challenges

The variety of spatial manifestations of informal settlements across the region is associated with the many different social dimensions to the problem. Notwithstanding these differences, several issues are important: notably, residents of informal settlements are often poor and disadvantaged, facing higher unemployment, social hardships and tenure insecurity.

Evidence suggests that demographic pressures from IDPs and vulnerable groups (e.g. the Roma population) are met by informal housing settlements (Council of Europe Development Bank et al. 2004). Figure V presents the disadvantaged groups in Belgrade residing in informal settlements, where young families with insufficient income for obtaining housing are the largest percentage at 35 per cent; next come refugees, who comprise 23 per cent; and the third largest demographic is the Roma population, with 18 per cent (UNECE, Vienna Conference 2004). Without financial resources and stable employment, many IDPs and refugees who moved to Belgrade to start a new life in 1995 and 1999 used Belgrade's informal housing potential as a possible solution.

In addition to the lack of access to schools and social services, peri-urban settlers generally do not hold secure land or housing tenure and face the potential threat of eviction. There are cases in the region where this might be different; one is Bishkek, where the city handed out unserviced land plots to some migrants (World Bank 2007). Security of tenure is not an issue in most cases in the older settlements in Montenegro, Serbia and the former Yugoslav Republic of Macedonia (in some, residents own the land); however, the lack of social infrastructure (e.g. schools, medical clinics and social services) perpetuates a spatial form of social exclusion.

In several countries, one of the worst consequences of living in an informal settlement is not the lack of title to the land or formal registration, but the fact that households are not eligible for unemployment benefits and social security payments and cannot place their children in local schools. While the former problem requires a comprehensive approach to the transformation of informal settlements that understands the crucial connection between physical interventions and economic and employment policies, the latter asks for a solution that takes accounts that the provision of basic services is an essential precondition for policy intervention. Informal settlements present significant social hardships for many of the residents, as the experiences from Bishkek indicate. Residents of the *novostroiki* without official registration (*propiski*) cannot vote or access social benefits and have limited access to schools. Preschools are not available and children must commute to more distant municipal schools (World Bank 2007).

In countries such as Albania, Azerbaijan, Bosnia and Herzegovina and Kyrgyzstan, as a result of rapid shifts in local economies and/or war, hundreds of thousands of relatively poor migrants or IDPs have moved to the capital cities. The new arrivals have settled in peri-urban areas, where they build houses on unserviced lots, squatting on private or public land. In most cases, poverty and deprivation are manifested in the poor quality of the housing being built as well as in the substandard pattern of urban development without any social or technical infrastructure. The example from Kamza illustrates some of these problems in the newly created neighborhoods (box 10).

Figure 5: Disadvantaged groups in Belgrade

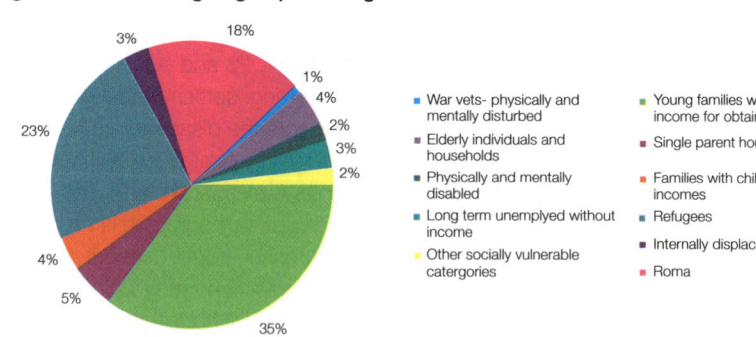

Source: UNECE, Vienna Conference 2004.

Box 10: Provision of social infrastructure and community facilities in Kamza, Albania

The Municipality of Kamza is one of Tirana's informal housing settlements, with over 90 per cent of all dwellings being constructed illegally. The settlement was primarily agricultural land in the early 1990s, but has grown substantially and has some 60,000 residents today (Besnik et al. 2003). Residents emigrated from the north-eastern regions of Albania with the hope of a better life and greater opportunities. Children (0–15 years) account for 40 per cent of the population. Adults have low levels of education and unemployment rates are high (around 50 per cent), with half of all households living below the poverty line (Municipality of Kamza 2002). The plan below shows the proposed land use and social infrastructure of Kamza, where the planning process is attempting to identify locations for much-needed public open space, schools and medical facilities. The average density of the area is 22 people per ha, while the average home is 119 m^2, twice the average for Tirana. Housing was initially built in the form of shacks and then upgraded as remittances were received and resources were found. While planning efforts and the work of non-governmental organizations such as Co-PLAN have boosted the confidence of residents and led to $110 million worth of investment, despite its limited revenue the local government in Kamza is involved in complex negotiations with squatters to gain land for social infrastructure.

Proposed land use and social infrastructure of southern areas of Kamza

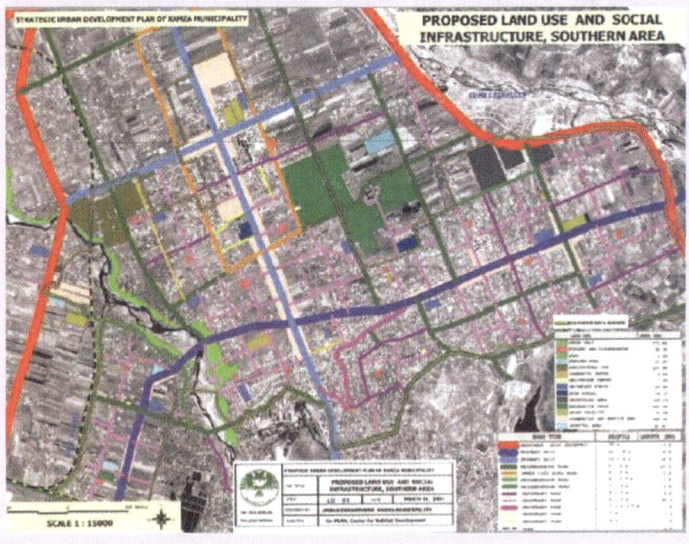

Source: Besnik et al. 2003.

3. The environmental challenges

The environmental challenges in informal settlements are associated with an unplanned use of land, which contributes to urban sprawl and deficient infrastructure. The situation also adversely affects the quality of life in the "formal" areas of the city, where urban run-off and downstream pollution from garbage and sewers that discharge directly in rivers pose serious environmental threats.

The infrastructure deficit in informal settlements is significant. Often illegal connections are the only means of access, which are unreliable and inefficient (Deda 2003). The illegal tapping lowers the efficiency of public utility companies and exposes regular users to power outages and water cut-offs. Since most residents in informal settlements do not pay the full price for infrastructure usage, the revenue is unable to support the growing demand for infrastructure improvement and extension. Correspondingly, the systems deteriorate, with serious economic and environmental consequences.

Data in table 4 present the infrastructure deficit in informal settlements in Tirana and Belgrade. The differences in access to essential services are significant when compared to the average for the city and the country as a whole. In the case of Roma settlements in Belgrade, the disadvantages are most pronounced. Only one quarter of all Roma settlements have access to sewerage, compared with 92 per cent for Belgrade city, and 47 per cent have piped water as compared to 98 per cent in the city on average. Even though data are lacking for other informal settlements in Belgrade, it can be assumed that a comparable lack of access to infrastructure might exist.

In addition to the infrastructure deficit, some settlements are directly exposed to environmental hazards associated with landslides, flooding, poor drainage, environmental pollution and exposure to various environmental hazards (box 11). These challenges create health risks for the residents, often children and women, and threaten their livelihoods.

In summary, informal settlement growth contributes to environmental degradation at many levels, inter alia: (a) erosion occurs from unpaved and undrained roadways in informal settlements; (b) residents without sewer systems increase pollution of local water sources through prohibited discharge; and (c) garbage is dumped in piles along roads or in local rivers. In some cases, informal settlements may create environmental hazards through development in natural reserves and protected areas. Examples of individual illegal constructions can be identified in coastal areas of Greece, Italy and Spain, and more so in Croatia. In most cases, such constructions in protected areas of high environmental or cultural value (e.g. archaeological sites, forests, coastlines) have been demolished (Pachic 2007, Panunzi 2007).

Table 4: Infrastructure deficit in informal settlements in Tirana and Belgrade (percentage)

Amenities	Informal settlements in Tirana	Tirana	Albania
Sewage	46	91	58
Piped water	41	95	56
Central heating	0	2	2
Access to electricity	68	97.3	86.5

Sources: UNECE 2002, Municipality of Tirana 2004.

Access to infrastructure (percentage of dwellings)	Roma settlements, Belgrade (2002)	Belgrade (1990/91)	Serbia
Sewage	25.2	92	78
Piped water	47.1	98	90
Central heating	N/A	49	28
Bath or shower	40	96	80

Sources: UNECE 2005, Tsenkova 2005.

Box 11: Environmental challenges in the peri-urban areas of Bishkek

Large internal migration flows in the Kyrgyz Republic in the past ten years have seen the emergence of new slums in the periphery of Bishkek—the *novostroiki*. Today, there are 47 precarious settlements of this type in the city. The largest has 4,800 land parcels, while the smallest have about 100. Many migrants often live in shoddy structures. Most of the settlements lack basic infrastructure services and are often located in areas where there are adverse environmental health-related impacts. One of the most populated slums, the Ak-Bosogo settlement, has very serious problems with water supply. Another populated area, Bakai-Ata, is located close to the ash dump of the Bishkek power and heating station, the source of heavy pollution. Even a slight wind lifts ash into the air, it covers all the houses and facilities in this residential area. Underground water is very close to the surface and causes destruction and flooding of houses during autumn and winter. Other settlements located in the lower part of the city are flooded after rains or melting snow, which regularly destroy the houses. Drainage systems are also collapsing due to the lack of funds to repair these systems.

Source: Rakisheva 2002, World Bank (2003).

CHAPTER 3

Changes in Governance and Informal Settlement Formation

Recognizing the economic, social and environmental challenges of informal settlements is an important step towards the design of different policies and practical solutions to their problems. Against the backdrop of rapid growth of informal settlements and/or the persistent presence of the "informal city" in some UNECE countries local, national and international policies have steadily evolved from repressive approaches aiming to eradicate slums to a growing recognition that inefficient housing, planning and land management systems aggravate these problems.

Improving living conditions must be a central focus of policies aiming to transform informal settlements. There is a need for housing-led interventions. However, in order to achieve a real effect for people in informal settlements, it is imperative to develop a new understanding of housing problems and a new integrated approach to housing policy. A national strategy for affordable and equal access to shelter for all and especially for the most vulnerable groups is very important. In this context, it is Governments that play a greater role by not only setting up appropriate regulatory frameworks, but by guaranteeing basic human rights and social protection for most vulnerable groups and a fair redistribution of wealth. Focusing merely on planning and land management systems cannot guarantee the achievement of these objectives.

Spatial planning and land management are usually understood as market-based regulatory tools to deal with public policy issues (e.g. housing) in countries with minimal role left for the social housing sector. It is well documented that addressing housing problems through planning mechanisms can further marginalize State-based approaches that provide low-income groups with affordable access to housing and land. If housing strategies, planning and land management are not coordinated or integrated into a general national land policy development framework, the implementation of wider social objectives may not be successful. There is solid evidence that planning regulations can increase housing prices and contribute to affordability problems. Furthermore, one problem informal settlements suffer from is to their exclusion from the spatial information strategies: another is the lack of social plans that integrating low-income residential development.

Box 12: Planning and land management constraints

The analytic and project work of the World Bank in a number of countries in the region points to the following common factors that influence illegal and informal development:

The absence of a recent "regulatory plan" (land use plan) and approved local regulations for land use. Plans may be outdated or incomplete. Many specifications like setbacks, width of major roads, floor-area ratio, and maximum heights may have to be negotiated project by project. This practice increases the cost of construction by causing lengthy delays and creates the impression of arbitrariness and opportunities for corruption. If the process is lengthy and unclear, many citizens may not have the knowledge, time or funds to follow the procedures.

The lack of funded municipal programmes to build primary infrastructure. Without the benefit of current infrastructure network plans, developers are obliged to build and finance on their own the off-site links between their units and the existing network, or extensions of the network. This leads to fragmentation of the system, making it uneconomic and expensive to maintain. Individuals may have no access to infrastructure or may "buy" illegal hook-ups.

The difficulty of acquiring undeveloped land, officially and legally, for construction. Most vacant land around cities is either encumbered by disputes over title or claims for restitution, or belongs to the government and is therefore not on the market. The ability of developers and individuals to find out about available land is hampered by incomplete records.

High transaction costs in the formal sector, complex processes and unresponsive institutions. In many countries the costs – in time, money and number of offices visited – to formally construct and register a building are substantial. Again, lengthy and confusing processes may "encourage" the informal sector, and the absence of strong enforcement by the responsible agencies also contributes.

Source: World Bank. 2007: 3.

It is now widely understood that migrants to the cities often end up as squatters in the informal settlements because the formal housing, land and even rental markets (if existing) are often unaffordable to these groups. Government support for housing solutions for the urban poor and disadvantaged groups has dwindled in the past decade, shifting the burden to local government, community groups and individual households. Following the move to a market-based economy much of the burden for housing naturally shifts to the private sector together with the local government. Illegal or informal land acquisitions, subdivisions and other self-help solutions are perhaps a natural coping mechanism for the poor urban migrants in the shanty towns, baracas and squatter neighborhoods. While in its new enabling role the State offers services and acts as a coordinator of policies and actions in the urban sphere, the market alone has not been able to provide affordable and adequate housing to all sectors of society. Informal settlements are a distinct manifestation of this change in governance. At its best, this enabling strategy has resulted in improved legislation, infrastructure and services as well as community driven attempts to regularize informal settlements. At its worst, it has turned a blind eye to their growth, constrained land supply, exacerbated corruption and forced the poor into spatially and socially isolated slums.

In a context of globalization and economic and political liberalization, the result of such policies has been the impoverishment of poor and disadvantaged groups in cities, and the explosive growth on the number and size of informal settlements in peri-urban areas with the combined effect of more complex and costly problems to be address. There is common acknowledgement that resolving the "urban problem" of informal settlements is related to the nexus of improved access to affordable land and housing as well as transparent and efficient planning regimes. A study of the World Bank (2007) on informal settlements in transition economies succinctly summarizes these issues (box 12).

1. Constraints in the land management and property registration system

Cities across the region, particularly in post-socialist countries, bear the main brunt of recent economic and social transformation – rapid urbanization, privatization of land and real estate and rapid introduction of new institutional, administrative and fiscal systems to manage urban development and massive illegal construction (Tsenkova 2006).

Constraints in the supply of land

In some post-socialist cities, in the absence of reformed regulatory instruments for strategic planning to guide land allocation and titling, privatized urban land was developed by individuals at a scale that challenged local government's ability to rapidly provide roads and technical infrastructure to hundreds of thousands of new residents. As a result of decentralization, municipalities in transition countries acquired many new functions without the adequate resources to fulfill their mandates. The challenges of performing local development and management under fiscal austerity in post-socialist cities are well documented. This financial weakness, coupled with the inability to borrow in capital markets and the dependence on central government transfers, drastically reduced the capacity of local governments to develop and maintain services. In cases where the city's population almost doubled, with a large share of new development being part of the "informal city', creating a huge infrastructure deficit, the financial commitment to servicing these areas was not commensurate with available local revenues and the fiscal regimes under which local authorities operate (e.g. in Bishkek). These fiscal constraints contributed to the shortage of serviced urban land for future development. However, in some countries of the UNECE region (e.g. in Italy), the excess of formal planning scattered among too many non-interacting actors, offices and sectors also effectively limited land supply.

Land privatization – and in some countries restitutions – has been implemented with various degrees of success. The scale of this land tenure transformation has been very dramatic, particularly in EECCA countries where private ownership over urban land was non-existent. For example, in the Russian Federation over 50 million people and legal entities have acquired private ownership of land. Some 129 million hectares of land, comparable to the area of Western Europe, has become privately owned just within four years (UNECE 2002). Together with legal and institutional developments related to land administration and valuation, privatization has facilitated the establishment of a modern land administration system. Implementation, however, is in most countries constrained by a multitude of problems, among them (a) incomplete land registration systems, (b) ineffective control due to inadequate institutional capacities, and (c) lack of transparency in land restitution and privatization.

In addition to a dynamic process of landownership transformation, the supply of land to achieve affordable housing objectives and the implementation of social housing programmes is often constrained by the lack of effective land-use planning to guide development. There is a need for land transfers that would provide private developers with cheap and serviced land in return for mixed-tenure housing development schemes. These land practices would enable people of low income to have equal and affordable access to different housing choices.

Fifteen years later, evidence suggested that most urban markets in post-socialist countries have become more fragmented, reflecting differential opportunities for development and profit. Land barter deals, very common at the start of the transition, have lost their attractiveness, but land prices in the capital cities and growth centres have increased. The myriad of ownership arrangements has created significant barriers for the efficient operation of urban land markets, contributing to the growth in land prices. In some EECCA countries, urban land is auctioned by municipalities, reportedly under procedures that are not very transparent.[9]

Incomplete land registration systems

Although most Governments have accelerated the development of modern land administration systems, a precondition for an effective land management, the coverage is often limited (e.g. in Montenegro up to 60 per cent) and the information on illegally

---

[9] There are presently two ways of allocating land for housing construction in Kyrgyzstan: land plots can be offered for sale on the open market or municipalities can sell land by auction. Despite the provisions of the land code, the actual process in the auction and sale of residential land plots can be considered non-transparent, resulting in a high levels of irregularity (IFC 2007).

constructed buildings is not incorporated. If informal constructions are not registered into the land administration system, there is no information available and no tool to allow sound decision-making and monitoring/inspection (Potsiou and Ioannidis 2006) In response to these challenges, some countries have allowed registration of illegally constructed buildings (without a building or occupancy permit accompanied with a special remark, e.g. in Georgia). Detection and registration are often still complicated processes that may be difficult in certain countries where nearly half of construction tends to be illegal or have some degree of informality. Detection and registration are essential tools to every democratic country with a free-economy economy. For them, there must be an efficient administration in place. Modern technical tools (e.g. automatic photogrammetric methods) can improve the efficiency of administration. In the Belgrade region, recent annual production by the formal market has been around 1,500 units per year, mostly for the upper segments of the market, while informal production averaged 50,000 a year. Furthermore, high fees and the difficulty of collecting the required documentation also contribute to the non-registration of land and housing.

The supply of serviced residential land constrained not only by local governments' lack of capacity to finance necessary infrastructure, but also by a cumbersome and lengthy approvals process. Typically, even if developers have access to land with a clear legal title, cash-constrained municipalities will shift infrastructure costs and demand various approvals and permits that reportedly take more than a year to collect. In some cases, e.g. in Greece, the title may be legally clear but the additional necessary permitting procedure is not easy due to unclear regulations and the lack of relevant spatial information (i.e. maps). In complicated cases, such as in areas without a city plan when special permits are needed (e.g. from agencies responsible for forest and archaeological sites), this procedure may take several years (Potsiou and Ioannidis, 2006).

Overall, this has led to high cost of serviced land on the market and fragmented the nature of land supply, particularly in large cities with higher demand. These developments are accompanied by the occupation of agricultural land in the urban periphery and the growth of informal settlements where the combination of inefficient administrative systems, the lack of necessary up-to-date maps with zoning regulations, and urban poverty create a cycle of economic and social deprivation.

It is in this context that the problem of informal settlements, particularly those created by the urban poor ought to be viewed. As Gabriel (2007) states,

There is a growing awareness that informal settlements, while undeniably a "problem" from an urban management point of view, may have to be seen rather as the only currently feasible "solution" in terms of social response to a deficit produced by largely artificial imbalances in the supply of land, by resulting escalation of land prices

While in some countries with established housing and land markets, spatial planning can be considered as a central policy tool, in others, particularly transitional countries with a long history and tradition of strong State support, spatial planning should be supplemented by other land policy instruments. The possible choices can be a direct affordable housing provision by the State, the establishment of "socially responsible" and formalized public-private partnerships, subsidies, elimination of inappropriate or unrealistic standards, etc. In certain contexts, social housing policy should be considered as a better strategy to achieve wider social goals.

Clearly, this is not a problem land administration agencies can solve alone, as it involves multiple levels of government and major policy choices. However, land administration can provide the tool for sound decision-making. The challenge is to develop a modern system of compatible ownership records and the use and value of land that closely resembles the complete state of affairs in the case of informal settlements. The ideal situation is when records are complete, current and accurate, and the system of records is designed to suit the human, financial, technical and communication resources available. At the same time, it is imperative to start planning with the information available, and to try to do so in the most effective way. Informal settlements call for immediate action, and in cases where there is an urgent need, modern technical tools should be used to collect all necessary information at a low-cost way that might establish the necessary conditions for taking immediate action. Also, the "learning by doing" approach may be appropriate in some situations. As technical managerial skills develop and more of the other resources become available, the level of sophistication of the record system should increase, as should the level of integration of these records with other land information. The multi-purpose character of the cadastre should be broadly advertised.

A further challenge when developing land records for informal settlements is that local social and political circumstances are not likely to change in a linear fashion. The accuracy and completeness of the information in the cadastre, including the information on informal settlements, is critical for a well-functioning real estate market and the protection of land and property rights. Availability of digital and accurate data sets, with common spatial reference concerning ownership, value, and use of land, is essential for efficient decisions of policymakers, planners, real estate developers and individuals. Decisions to legalize informal settlements may be impossible to implement without this information. For example, the Real Estate Registration Project supported by the World Bank helped to regularize 500,000 illegal constructions in Kyrgyzstan. This was done as part of the ongoing systematic registration process and resulted in a significant growth in the use of property as collateral for credit. During 2005, Gosregister registered the equivalent of $418 million in mortgages.

2. Constraints in the planning and approval system

Planning has a critical role in defining the appropriate strategies to respond to the existing informal settlement challenge. It is an essential ingredient of the legal framework for regularization and upgrading. Planning is often delegated to the local level, and it is important to ensure a high level of citizen participation during the regularization process. The critical constraints related to these responsibilities are associated with the lack of institutional capacity and resources to effectively plan and manage development at the local level. Countries have decentralized functions to municipal authorities by enacting laws on local self-government. Decentralization seems to have amounted to a transfer of responsibilities to the local level, often without a commensurate transfer of human and financial resources. For example, in some countries the revenue from real estate taxation is not returned to the local authorities for re-investment in the same areas, but it is used by the central government. This central policy may still work well for certain developing countries allowing the central government to provide smoother infrastructure development and social housing policy in the whole country and to avoid the creation of extreme differences between very rich and very poor neighborhoods. Given the problem of limited finances and capacity to invest in essential infrastructure and services, local governments in some cases lack the human capacity to guide the planning process, enforce compliance, and create the detailed plans and building permits. In such cases, the private sector has a role to play. Compilation and implementation of the necessary spatial data infrastructure (cadastral, hydrological, geological, and planning and regeneration projects, etc.) may be commissioned to the private sector under the supervisory approval and control of the local authorities. Real estate property taxation may be directed to the local authorities and reinvested. Until there is some real estate there to tax, however, local authorities should be funded by the central government. Legalization of informal settlements may offer one way to bring extra revenue to the local authorities. Owners of informal settlements should contribute to the costs for the services and the necessary improvements for their neighborhoods (Potsiou and Mueller 2007).

There is a need for a change in the countries' spatial planning practices. Planning system should now take into consideration the ways different potential players can be integrated into spatial planning processes. Their capacity to participate and influence spatial decision-making processes must be strengthened and formalized. While there is a need for local spatial planning practices, the connected-ness between the local and national levels must not be lost. A vision for local development should be integrated into national strategies, just as national objectives should be translated into a given local context to ensure better responses to the needs of local people.

Inefficient planning and land management at the local level

The lack of reliable tools such as spatial data infrastructures (cadastral maps, hydrological and geological maps, zoning plans, etc.) frequently causes serious delays in the development of spatial plans and hampers strategic direction for future development and growth, particularly in areas under pressure for development. Incomplete registration of property rights and mass illegal/informal development in particular quickly renders regulatory plans obsolete or irrelevant in the real world of real estate development. In some countries where informal settlements have sprung up over the last decade, plans are either outdated or simply non-existent. Box 13 illustrates these challenges in Montenegro.

Box 13: Planning constraints in Montenegro

In Montenegro, planning is done at three different levels, corresponding to a hierarchical structure of planning and approval process: spatial plans, general urban plans and detailed urban plans. While spatial plans exist for 83 per cent of the territory, the general urban plans cover about 5 per cent of the territory in most of the 21 municipalities, while detailed urban plans exist in about one third of the municipalities with general urban plans. The spatial distribution of this coverage is presented in the map below. In the absence of detailed urban plans, planning and development permits are either delayed or issued on the basis of partial amendments of the old regulatory plan in a rather arbitrary way.

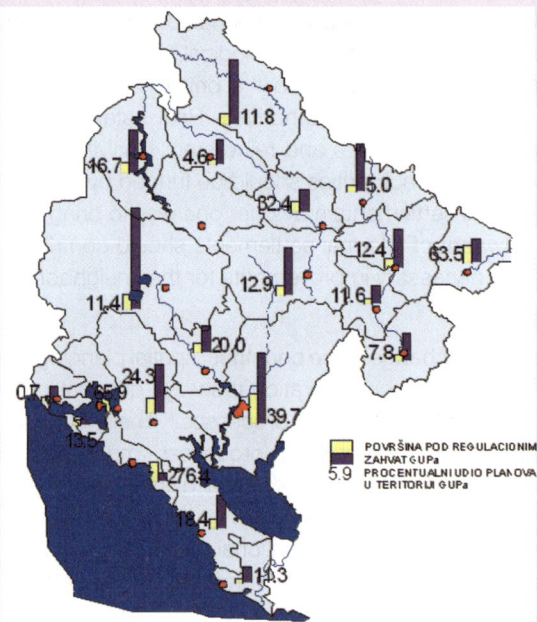

Source: Müller and Lješković 2007.

Bureaucratic planning procedures

Rigid and inflexible implementation of the zoning plans are regarded as significant barriers in transition countries as well as in many UNECE developed countries. There is a limited legal basis for spatial planning and physical development. Old master plans dating from the Soviet period in many cases have not been updated; often, due to the lack of the necessary legislation and means to ensure the validity of legislation, new construction projects and changes in land use are approved without regard to urban development documentation. At present, there are neither the competent personnel nor the economic resources available to carry out master planning for all areas where this is required. Most of the municipalities have resorted to amendments of older plans and ad hoc changes responding to development pressures. In Georgia, for example, the last development plans were elaborated in the 1970s and 1980s. The term for validity of most long-term master plans of Soviet period expired only in 2000. This expiry date was extended to 2004 with the Presidential Decree (of February 2002) on Prolongation of the Terms of Validity of Master Plans. In other cases, controversial informal settlement development has challenged the ability of local governments to approve the new generation of plans. For example, Tirana has six plans, but none have been approved.

In addition to the constraints created by the lack of detailed regulatory plans, local governments face the challenge of regulating development in the absence of clear legal and technical frameworks with a high degree of operational applicability. Frequent changes in normative and legal bases, the lack of normative standards for enforcement and new construction laws, standards and norms are much more significant constraints for the small and often underfunded departments that deal with building and occupancy permits. Furthermore, a complex and less transparent system for obtaining permits and licenses for construction contributes to delays and abuse. In Montenegro, for example, a recent study demonstrated that a permit to build 1,000 m^2 was conditional upon 15 approvals, three certificates and two official statements from 15 different institutions, which were delineated in 14 laws and a number of bylaws and municipal decisions. Even more complex are the legal stipulations regarding administrative fees to obtain the necessary documents, which might range from €2,000–30,000 in addition to a contribution for communal fees (infrastructure burden) around 5 per cent of the construction costs. In Greece, construction is also permitted in areas without a city plan under certain regulations. This has resulted in many regions with unplanned (if not necessarily illegal) development, which includes both legal and illegal construction. When the unplanned development becomes dense, it is a common practice to put in place an urban regeneration project. It is estimated that in order to regenerate an area of 300 ha, one would need nine months for the cadastral survey (including objection periods); 16 months for the compilation of a city plan in two stages (analysis and proposal, 12 months, and supporting geological study and survey of natural water drainage network, 4 months); and 12 months for the implementation of the city plan (even if two or three revisions are required). Theoretically, it takes an average of three years to regenerate an area of 300 ha. In reality, however, it is rare for a regeneration project to be completed under six years; the average time is 8–10 years (Potsiou and Dimitriadi 2008).

It is not surprising that such cumbersome and expensive procedures discourage investors, in particular small ones, and unintentionally act as incentives for illegal construction. Inappropriate regulations, unclear rules and the difficult language of official documents, as well as the lack of transparency in the system of granting building permissions, have all become too costly to comply with, especially for the most vulnerable groups. It is necessary that cumbersome regulatory frameworks be reconsidered and regulatory frameworks become more inclusive, enabling transparent systems supporting sustainable development of places and people's well-being. The challenge for informal settlements to comply with formal regulations can be addressed, for instance, by reconsidering inappropriate and excessive standards (e.g. o lower entry standards) or facilitating some forms of local self-regulation.

Growing problems with illegal construction

Box 14: Difficulties in coping with illegal construction in Georgia

In Tbilisi, the lack of spatial plans and adequate institutional structures to enforce effective planning and building control have resulted in massive illegal occupation of land and illegal construction. The most common features of illegal construction in Tbilisi are the absence of design, planning documents and construction permits. Presidential Decree No. 874 on Activities for the Detection of the Illegalities which took place in the Use of the State Land Fund 1995–2000 and their Elimination, issued in June 2002, instructs the Ministry of Justice to impose responsibility by the Criminal Law for illegal occupation of land and to submit the appropriate project.

This decree had so far little impact, however. Regulations remain necessary. The Government should apply those regulations that they can, and incentives and alternative options should be provided as well. Absence of legal titles and building permits is not considered to be "adequate documentation" if this is a massive phenomenon. In order for such constructions to be demolished, it has to be proved that there is an opportunity for their integration. Legislation is still being prepared in Parliament on the legalization of informal buildings; i.e. the legalization of a construction if the building qualifies for a building permit and can be certified as fit for use. This is a feasible democratic tool that takes into consideration the current situation and needs. Examples in Tbilisi indicate that illegal construction by owners and developers can result in problematic extensions posing security threats in seismic conditions and affecting the quality of life in residential areas; those constructions should be improved before any legalization. According to the Main Construction Inspectorate, in 2004 out of 277 inspected sites, 34 per cent were illegal and another third had no construction permit.

Source: UNECE, 2007.

The lack of detailed regulatory urban plans and cumbersome procedures to obtain building permits contribute to the growing problem of illegal construction. In a number of countries, this may reinforce the existing tendency to build housing – often single-family – in stages, without necessary documentation or the intention to legalize the development. In some countries, the simple absence of effective framework to control illegal development might be aggravating the situation, as the example of Georgia indicates (box 14).

Box 15: City profile: Belgrade

After the dismantlement of the Socialist Federal Republic of Yugoslavia in the early 1990s, the Republic of Serbia absorbed an important flow of displaced people fleeing the numerous conflicts in the region; first influxes from Croatia and Bosnia and Herzegovina between 1992 and 1997 raised the number of refugees to 550,061 in 1997 (2005 UNHCR Statistical Yearbook), and the violent events in the southern region of Kosovo (Serbia) increased the number of IDPs to 267,500 in 2000 (2005 UNHCR Statistical Yearbook). In 2005, Serbia was still the country hosting the largest number of refugees and IDPs in Europe. Even though the Government of Serbia granted the Serb citizenship to 300,000 of those refugees, problems inherent with their unstable situation remain. In fact, this rapid and unexpected influx of population into Serbian territory caused long-term stresses to the country's housing system, as most of the displaced people have had no choice but to resort to informal and illegal housing.

In 2003, the Belgrade Urbanism Institute determined that there were about 145,000 people living in informal settlements in Belgrade, classified under four main categories. The majority of informal dwellers live in compact informal housing scattered over 34 zones around the city and in 18 low density informal settlements in the surrounding area. Another 25,000 live in worse conditions in 64 unsanitary settlements and more than 20 urban slums (defined as "poor and unsanitary settlements" by Serbian legislation). Half of these settlements are found in central areas – under bridges, near public transportation and in dumps (Urban Planning Institute of Belgrade 2004).

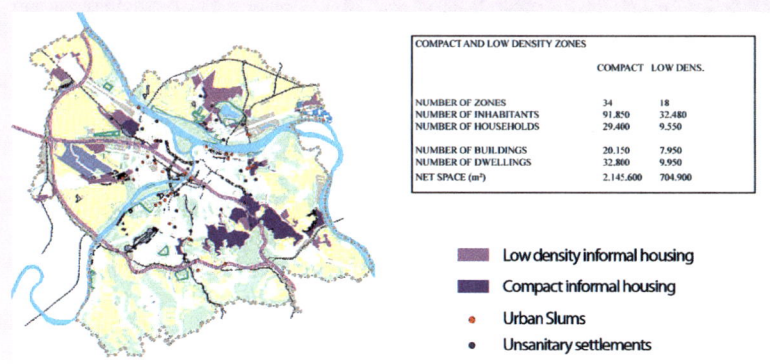

COMPACT AND LOW DENSITY ZONES		
	COMPACT	LOW DENS.
NUMBER OF ZONES	34	18
NUMBER OF INHABITANTS	91.850	32.480
NUMBER OF HOUSEHOLDS	29.400	9.550
NUMBER OF BUILDINGS	20.150	7.950
NUMBER OF DWELLINGS	32.800	9.950
NET SPACE (m²)	2.145.600	704.900

Low density informal housing

Compact informal housing

Urban Slums

Unsanitary settlements

Faced with the rapid growth of those informal settlements, the Serbian Government and the Belgrade municipality have taken a series of measures to address the problem mainly through legal action. Laws and policies passed since 1993 have progressively evolved from repressive approaches (e.g. the Decision on Legalization of Illegally Constructed Building, adopted by the city of Belgrade in 1993, the Law on Special requirements for the Issuing of Building Permit or Certificate of Occupancy for Specific Buildings or the Amending Law to the Construction Law) aiming at stopping illegal construction to a growing recognition that better planning and land management and improved housing conditions could provide a solution to the problem. The Planning and Construction Law, for instance, provides new opportunities for legalization through plan reviews and the preparation of temporary building rules, with simultaneous registration of illegal construction. However, despite a number of laws, the regularization and legalization process of informal settlements in Serbia remains quite difficult due to the transition phase that Serbian cadastre and land registration system are undergoing.

Today, the registration of buildings and land are performed through either the Land Cadastre, the Land Book, the Real Estate Cadastre or the older and rarely utilized Title Deed Book. Land Cadastre covers the whole territory of Serbia and is run and maintained by the Governmental Geodetic Authority. The Land Cadastre contains data on land parcels with regard to their position, shape, area and category. The cadastral map is not in digital form. The Land Book is a public register that records actual rights on real estate, including land, buildings and special part of buildings. The Land Book was introduced in 1930 with adoption of the Law on Land Book, and still applies today. In 1988, the Serbian Government decided to merge the two into the new unified Real Estate Cadastre unifying Land Cadastre and Land Book. This process is still in progress and both Land Cadastre, Land Book and Real Estate Cadastre still operate together, but the implementation of a Real Cadastre System is hampered by a lack of financial resources and inadequate educational and training of personnel (UNECE 2006). Such overlapping of land and buildings registration system does not facilitate the legalization of informal settlements.

The Urban Planning Institute of Belgrade's project of urban integration of Padina, a compact informal settlement in the southeast of Belgrade, provides a good example of difficulties the institution encountered to legalize and integrate informal settlements. In 2004, the Urban Institute started an integration plan for Padina based on a legalization process including cadastral registration, spatial planning and integration of the neighborhood into a wider and long term urban master plan.

After a first phase of spatial and urban planning, to design the new layout of the streets and to organize the public spaces, a legalization process for the buildings and land plots was carried out. However, difficulties related to the coordination of the land and buildings registration in the Cadastre, the Land Book and the Real Estate Cadastre left the registration of all the buildings incomplete.

As a result, the situation in Padina, as in most informal settlements around Belgrade, is currently in deadlock because of this difficult transitional phase in land administration processes.

3. Constraints in the housing provision system

The growth of informal settlements maybe contributing to constraints in the supply of serviced land, complex bureaucratic approval procedures and inconsistent legal restrictions on development, not to mention expenses and taxes imposed by the State. While these may be factors in many countries in the region, especially when the land administration and planning policies fail to respond to changing realities, failure to address the demand for low-cost housing or shelter for the urban poor undoubtedly are the most important factor underlying informal settlement growth. Although its manifestations in different countries and cities might be different—from squatting in shanty towns and slums to overcrowding in substandard inner-city neighborhoods—the primary reason is the growing affordability problems and the lack of tenure choice.

Housing reforms in the UNECE region in the past decade have promoted policies to reassert market forces and reduce State intervention. With respect to housing provision, they have emphasized deregulation, private-sector involvement and demand-based subsidies. While the overall goal of these reforms has been to improve the economic and social efficiency of housing systems, various responses demonstrate that housing affordability is becoming more problematic. The housing sector in the countries with a significant share of informal housing suffers from imbalances caused by the lack of rental production (public or private) for low-income households, the spiraling costs of urban land and housing in growth areas, and limited support for vulnerable groups (e.g. the elderly, displaced populations, minority groups and the socially disadvantaged) to access housing of decent quality. It is therefore not surprising that in some urban areas experiencing rapid growth, the numbers of inadequately housed low-income people are increasing and/or the urban poor tend to house themselves directly or through informal contractors, outside the legal and planning framework.

Lack of tenure choice

Tenure choice is vital for long-term housing market stability and access to adequate and affordable housing. Most countries in the region have a polarized tenure structure with excessively high share of owner occupation. Entry into owner occupation is expensive, even if it may lead to significant financial benefits over the long term. With few alternative options, new households may be pushed into owner occupation when financially stretched. In a number of countries (e.g. Canada, France, Germany and the United States) a large share of private rental housing provides options for labour mobility. Tenure choices are much wider in Austria, Denmark, Finland and Sweden, thanks to a balanced tenure structure offering a ladder of opportunities ranging from social to private renting to homeownership. By contrast, in several European countries the rental option has been severely curtailed (e.g. Greece, Italy and Spain). The rental sector in some countries in EECCA is non-existent and in Central and South-Eastern Europe it remains only in a handful of countries where ongoing privatization continues to reduce its share.

Figure 6: Homeownership in the UNECE region, 2004

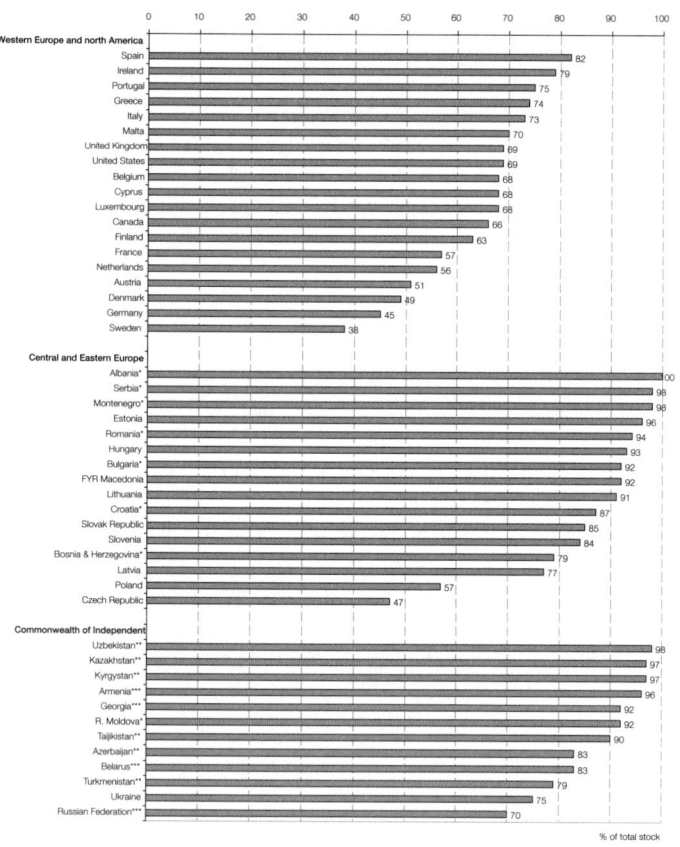

Sources: Author's estimates based on data from: MoIIRC for the EU-25, *Tsenkova 2005 for South-Eastern Europe and **UNECE Database and Duncan 2005 for the Commonwealth of Independent States.

Homeownership has grown steadily in most countries, particularly in countries in transition. In most countries, owner occupation exceeds 90 per cent, which is well above the 65 per cent average in Western Europe (figure 6). In fact, some of the poorest countries in the UNECE region have the highest rates of homeownership. Although some of this housing might actually function as private rentals, responding to pressures from migration and labour market adjustment, the tenure structure in the post-communist bloc is quite polarized, leaving only a small and residual sector of publicly owned social housing.

The processes of globalization and welfare state retrenchment have resulted in the adoption of new market-based housing strategies with a focus on a private market and homeownership. Such pro-ownership housing discourse has become so dominant that alternative perspectives to deal with the housing issue have been significantly marginalized or ignored. Furthermore, it is often argued that the recent global strategy for "adequate shelter for all and sustainable human settlements" has also been dominated by the idea of a private housing market. The lack of alternative housing choices has had significant implications for low-income groups, who have found themselves struggling to adapt to the standards and rules of the "ownership society". Such a situation only reinforces social exclusion and marginalization of low-income groups, especially the most vulnerable ones living in informal settlements. As the recent sub-prime mortgage crisis has shown, a critical moment has arrived for Governments to introduce a new pluralist approach to housing. This should provide marginalized groups with equal and affordable access to housing.

Growing affordability problems

Poverty across the UNECE region is manifesting itself through the growing number of people on welfare, rising homelessness and a general shortage of affordable housing, particularly in urban areas. In Western Europe and North America, housing policies have emphasized the importance of financial instruments – mortgage insurance, tax incentives and demand assistance to target groups – to facilitate access and choice. However, due to price inflation and higher rates of homeownership, the gap between income and entry costs has continued to increase for low-income households, making affordable housing of decent quality more difficult to obtain. In transition countries, rapid price increases in the last five years, coupled with high unemployment and higher interest rates on mortgages, have excluded more than 80 per cent of new households from the housing market. The previous housing shortage has been replaced by a shortage of affordable housing, suggesting a deepening housing crisis. Meanwhile, demand-based subsidies to low-income renters have failed to keep pace with the rising housing costs. In most UNECE countries, such assistance is non-existent and where it has been launched (e.g. Czech Republic, Estonia, Latvia, Poland and Romania), it only reaches a small number of households and is grossly inadequate (Lux 2003).

Figure 7: Households experiencing financial difficulties due to housing costs, 2004

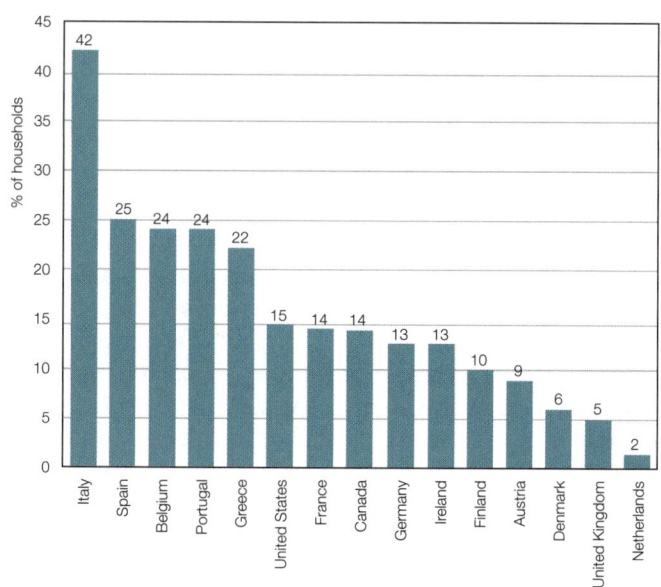

Note: Data for Canada: CMHC 2007; for United States: JCHS 2007.
Source: Eurostat, 2007.

Affordability of housing remains the fastest-growing and most pervasive housing challenge in the UNECE region. Housing costs have increased, with significant implications for access to adequate and affordable housing, particularly for vulnerable groups. The data in figure 7 present the share of households experiencing significant financial difficulties due to housing costs across the region. In four countries — Belgium, Greece, Portugal and Spain – one quarter of the households are financially stressed. In Italy this share is exceptionally high, having reached 42 per cent in 2004. While the data are limited, it appears that countries with higher homeownership rates and limited tenure choice tend to have a higher share of households experiencing affordability problems. Furthermore, the situation appears to be more problematic in urban areas where higher prices for housing and concentration of poverty create cumulative disadvantages.

Limited provision of social housing

While affordability constraints are growing, less social housing is being provided for low income households. In Canada and the United States, a handful of local governments have had the political will to overcome some of the barriers to developing affordable housing. Developing housing for extremely low-income households is difficult without multiple subsidies and complex financing packages. While a lot of the projects aim at private or non-profit sector involvement for a new provision of social housing, without capital subsidies to fill the gap between what low-income renters can pay and the rents needed to cover development costs, programmes cannot adequately serve the poor. Furthermore, the combination of higher construction and operating costs, along with stagnant or even declining rents tied to household income limits, can undermine the fundamental viability of affordable housing projects. In this context, it is not surprising that new social housing is not being provided in most countries across the region. Figure 8 suggests that in countries where the sector is significant, there is an ongoing commitment to maintain adequate supply. The data presents the share of social housing in each country and the new social housing built in 2004 as a share of total new construction. Austria (30 per cent), Denmark (20.7 per cent) and Sweden (16 per cent) have the highest rates of new social housing production, followed by Finland, the Netherlands and the United Kingdom, with rates in the range of 12 per cent. It is interesting to note that several countries (Czech Republic, Poland, and Slovakia) have initiated new social housing programmes in recognition of their importance for marginalized groups in society.

Figure 8: Social housing: existing stock and rates of new construction, 2004

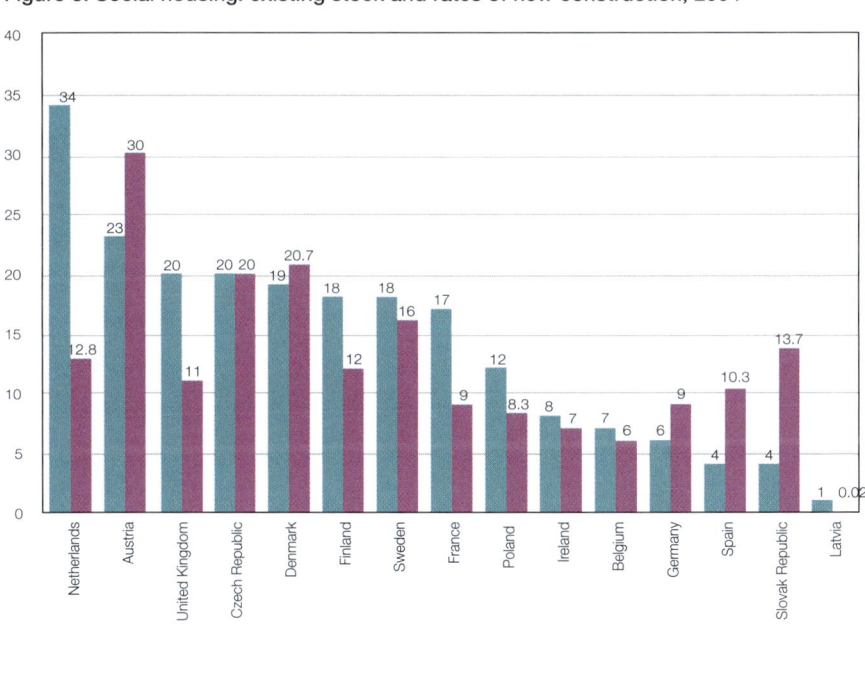

Source: MolIR, 2006.

CHAPTER 4

Towards inclusive urban development:
An opportunity to be seized

Review of different manifestations of informal settlements in the UNECE region indicates a number of contributing factors: rapid urbanization, displacement of vulnerable people, dysfunctional land management and planning systems, and persistent shortage of affordable housing. The ways different countries come to terms with the existing illegal and informal development as well as the ways they find to prevent such development in the future differ, as they depend upon history, politics, economics and social development (and the type of informal settlements). Increasing decentralization and changes in governance in many countries will also impact these choices, since solutions will require action at all levels of government, leadership from municipal administrations and the mobilization of residents of informal settlements.

The type and extent of informal settlement formation vary from country to country and from city to city within the same country, according to local conditions and existing planning and land management frameworks. Many countries in the region (e.g. Greece, Italy and Spain) have attempted to address the challenges of informal settlements in the last 20 (or even 30 or 60) years through: (a) privatizing land to refugees and providing housing to the poor (after the Second World War); (b) more effective control and regularization of territorial development; (c) decentralized planning and land management; (d) more systematic education at all levels (e.g. university graduate engineers, lawyers, registers, judges, technical practitioners, local authorities, the public and the media) in land tenure aspects; (e) addressing construction and civil engineering issues; (f) professional training in building inspection; and (g) planning and neighborhood upgrading. Significant attention was paid to increasing public awareness of environmental issues, of the benefits of following the technical specifications and regulations in construction, and of the risks of being informal. Significant research has been pursued in the academia and the public and private sectors on these issues.

In some transition countries where the informal settlement phenomenon is relatively new, efforts have focused on the general improvement of land registration systems and the development of a real estate cadastre to secure tenure and facilitate real estate market and property transactions. A further goal has been more effective land policy implementation. The role of these land policies, when coordinated with planning and zoning tools, may be very important for eliminating informality, since the authorities can monitor ownership rights and land use, plan more effectively and eliminate illegal occupation of public land. While these measures have not explicitly targeted the informal settlement problem, in general terms they have provided better spatial data infrastructure for urban planning and management with respect to general compliance with the existing planning and building regulations.

This chapter focuses on policy measures and interventions addressing specifically the "urban problems" of informal settlements, notably the following major types of policy intervention:

- Formalization and legalization
- Regularization and upgrading
- Resettlement and reallocation
- Alternative housing systems for informal settlements
- Substandard inner-city housing: urban renewal and regeneration strategies

The search for policy solutions to address illegal settlements is clearly multifaceted and multidimensional. Various projects and urban development programmes have been implemented in countries such as Greece, Italy, Portugal and Spain in the last 20 years. Although current needs may differ, these countries offer an important source of good practices for others in the region facing similar challenges. Solutions range from legalization and inclusion in formal urban plans to regularization and provision of essential social (schools, medical clinics) to technical infrastructure (safe roads, public transit, water and sewer) to resettlement programmes employing social housing. While these solutions illustrate different aspects of the policy continuum, they also entail significant political will and financial commitment on the part of central and local State institutions. It should also be remembered that examples from recent years in Southern Europe differ widely in nature from those currently developing in EECCA and Central and South-Eastern Europe. Results in these cases have been mixed, and new solutions, alternatives and approaches are needed to address the current informal settlement problems in the region.

1. Formalization and legalization

Formalization of informal settlements has been implemented widely in all countries across the region or is in the process of being so. The formalization approach emphasizes the integration of informal land and housing markets within the sphere of the formal economy. Ensuring the security of land tenure throughout de facto protection against eviction and de jure formalization of land tenure for informal settlements is one of the major challenges for government (Durand-Lasserve, 2007). International donors and Governments have also extensively promoted land titling programmes as a means of increasing tenure security, improving access to formal credit and reducing poverty (Payne 2007).

Such approaches are part of an urban development strategy combining privatization and cost recovery for urban services. The legalization of the unintended status quo is driven by efforts to capture public revenue (e.g. taxes on land and economic activities, other land related fees or revenue from penalties). The need for tighter integration of legalization processes with objectives to stabilize large urban communities through potential social and infrastructure upgrading programmes has been recently acknowledged. Some have argued that limited market-based strategies aiming at urban development simply formalize the urban land market, but do not pay the necessary attention to the negative social effects of such practices.

Legalization strategies essentially support the Global Plan of Action of the Habitat II Declaration, which emphasized the need for ensuring access to land (where land is recognized as a basic human right):

> Access to land and legal security of tenure are strategic prerequisites for the provision of adequate shelter for all and for the development of sustainable human settlements affecting both urban and rural areas; it is also one way of breaking the vicious circle of poverty. In order to ensure an adequate supply of serviceable land, Governments…should recognize and legitimize the diversity of land delivery mechanisms; decentralize land management responsibilities and provide capacity-building programmes that recognize the role of key interested parties, where appropriate; [and] explore innovative arrangements to enhance security of tenure, other than full legislation, which may be too costly and time-consuming in certain situations.

> Durand-Lasserve (2006) identifies recent trends in understanding security of tenure issues by international organizations. "Urban actors are changing their strategy regarding secure tenure, with impact on cities' administration, urban governance and sustainable urban development." Tenure regularization policies are being shaped within a new conceptual framework: moving away from security of tenure based on landownership and titling programmes towards a more comprehensive approach focusing on informal settlements' social and economic integration of. This new approach recognizes security of tenure based on legal pluralism and a mixed land market.

In 2000, the Global Campaign for Secure Tenure was introduced and a new unit on Land and Tenure of Shelter Branch of UN-Habitat was established. The Campaign

Forms part of Habitat's commitment to contribute to the emergence of a new urban paradigm. The extension of secure tenure is but one part of an integrated approach to improving access of the urban poor, not only to improve shelter and...basic services, but also to informal and formal employment opportunities, as well as direct political representation.... The Campaign is designed to spearhead a shelter strategy that is pragmatic, affordable and implementable (Durand-Lasserve 2006: 6)

The following are the practices that have been developed to translate these global processes into various national contexts. Overall, responses to legalization differ according to local context, e.g. types of informal settlements, Governments' political orientation, and pressure from civil society in general and from concerned communities in particular. In some countries (e.g. Croatia and Montenegro), legalization is carried out as an integral part of renewed efforts to develop statutory plans regulating development at the local level. In other countries (e.g. Albania and Serbia), legalization of informal settlements is addressed through special legislation, although implementation has been limited. Albania's Legalization Law, adopted in 2007, provides special provisions for the informal settlements of the poor to legalize their tenure status despite violation of existing planning and construction legislation. Other countries in the region have similar strategies, although progress in implementation might be uneven (box 15 and 16).

In countries where large-scale legalization has been implemented (e.g. Turkey), studies point to a number of problems (Durand-Lasserve 2006; UN-HABITAT 2003; 2005c), as follows:

Technical and financial. Legalization programmes proceed extremely slowly as a result of lengthy and costly procedures of plot measuring and registration. Legality also proves expensive for many poor urban residents despite the subsidies allocated for the process. Registration fees for land and property titles, in addition to future taxes and fees for services, may be beyond the capacity of poor households which opted for illegality in the first place.

Political and administrative: Legalization requires an appropriate administrative and regulatory environment, one adapted to (a) the identification of households entitled to tenure regularization, (b) the resolution of land related conflicts and (c) the allocation procedures of rights on land and housing. At the institutional level, implementation of legalization policies requires specialized institutions and political and administrative reforms. At the administrative level, implementation and enforcement of legalization policies can prove difficult. Major problems encountered in the implementation process are the result of the passive resistance of the intermediate-level officials in charge of land management and legalization, and the residents of informal settlements themselves.

Furthermore, when large-scale allocation of property titles to households living in informal settlements has been made possible, it has often resulted in intensified pressure from the formal property market within the settlement as well as an increase in the cost of services, both of which have tended to exclude the poorest sections of the population (Devecigil 2005). These harmful if unintended consequences suggest the need for critical analysis of the positive and negative outcomes of increased formalization, i.e. a commodification of the urban tenure process, as evidence from Turkey suggests (box 17).

Local and central government officials in the western Balkans, where informal settlements are a major challenge in large cities, recognize that bringing the status quo into legality while doing away with the most unacceptable instances of infringement and preventing future illegal development is a priority. The Stability Pact and UN-HABITAT have initiated a regional support programme aimed at improving the capacity for urban development and housing in Albania, Bosnia and Herzegovina, Croatia, Kosovo (Serbia), Montenegro, the former Yugoslav Republic of Macedonia and Serbia. The programme has sustained a policy dialogue in the subregion on alternatives to deal with the growing phenomenon of informal settlement formation. However, the actions to realize the commitments of the Vienna Declaration have been rather limited. The lead consultant for the programme highlights the interrelated reasons for this situation:

> Municipal authorities are especially constrained in devising city-wide planning responses to the problem not just because of limitations in their capacities to carry out comprehensive strategic planning exercises and city-wide land management plans, but often also because of structural problems in the normative framework, often insufficient access to crucial land and property information bases and inadequate equipment. Ad hoc, limited-scale interventions of upgrading and limited resettlement are therefore the norm. Meanwhile the same pattern of illegal occupation in all its different manifestations continues and current interventions seem unable to provide a long-term answer to the unmet social demand for cheap land and housing (cited in Gabriel 2007:11).

In other parts of the region, government (central and local) has attempted to legalize the *novostroiki* areas to a very limited extent. The government's role has been largely reactive, not proactive. In some other countries, particularly those facing the challenges of post-conflict land and housing management problems, no action has been taken. At the same time, the scale of the informal settlements in some cities is overwhelmingly compromising future development and growth. Based on the above evidence, the following findings about disadvantages and advantages of this approach become evident.

Titling is important for two reasons: the personal interests of the occupiers (e.g. security of tenure, protection against forced eviction, domestic conflicts, marital separation, inheritance, problems with neighbors, access to an address and to forms of credit); and the interest of the city as a whole, since legal titling can contribute to the stabilization of land markets and allow for more rational and better articulated forms of public intervention" (Fernandes, 2004). However, there have been many critical responses about the limited recognition of tenure security. A conventional market-based approach to legalization that prioritizes the ownership occupation often has negative implications for people's lives and the sense of community in informal settlements. There is also a danger of displacement of the marginalized groups through market processes, which only reinforces the patterns of socio-spatial exclusion. It is also frequently reported that legalization is implemented as a separate process with little connection to upgrading programmes. A main concern is that focusing on individual freehold titles marginalizes other legal and institutional mechanisms supporting collective responses to social problems. There still exists much potential for alternative processes, and these should also be recognized by the different key actors involved in informal settlements upgrading, especially private institutions (e.g. banks and builders).

Many experts argue that title does not necessary make people safer with regard to their future investment in housing; the perception of people themselves about their tenure security plays a major role. However, guaranteed equal, safe and affordable access to occupation is fundamental when dealing with the deprivation of informal settlements. Secure tenure is a key asset to tackling poverty, motivating wealth accumulation and supporting the livelihoods of marginalized groups. Otherwise, people are not motivated to invest in their material assets or home-based enterprises, and such a situation only reinforces deprivation. Insecure tenure rights have negative implications for achieving improved living conditions and affordable access to shelter for all. They also have also a negative effect on long-term planning and distort prices for land and services provision. Insecurity of tenure increases the possibility of the eviction of vulnerable people. Services in informal settlements are also provided informally, so people usually pay the "poverty premium". In this environment, the benefits they consider while building their unauthorized housing are significantly reduced.

Security of tenure must be considered as part of an integrated and comprehensive approach. Legalization is a prerequisite for further steps in tenure upgrading and regularization. As part of an integrated approach, security of land tenure is considered as closely linked to adequate and affordable access to shelter. A main concern must be a provision of secure access to land and housing that recognizes tenure formalization as an incremental process. Such an approach should give marginalized groups and others time to understand the process and to benefit from title upgrading.

Incremental tenure formalization with a key focus on housing as a basic human right can help bridge the gap between the necessity of a formal system of shelter supply and the resources of the population. Certain approaches have been suggested in response to the criticism of the ownership-based legalization which prevent marginalized groups from accessing affordable and adequate housing. There are some cases of legalization with intention of providing social housing rights without giving up public land, as well as to provide an effective security of tenure within certain legal and urban planning conditions that minimize the likelihood of beneficiaries being "forced" to leave under market pressures. Innovative land tenure regularization approaches should recognize housing rights and security of tenure and should promote socio-spatial integration of informal settlements.

Findings also point out the problem that beneficiaries of legalization programmes do not have sufficient knowledge and understanding of the process. It is thus important that regularization programmes are complemented with education and capacity-building.

Box 16: Legalization in Tirana

ALUIZNI is the responsible national Agency for Legalization and Urbanization of Illegal Constructions and Settlements. Its work is to put together proposals for approving the legalization of illegal settlements in Tirana. ALUIZNI has prepared a pilot legalization process of an area of 55 ha. The area is being processed for a complete digitalized documentation containing not less than 30 characters for each property to be registered. The first legalization permits were granted during February 2007. The registration of properties will follow the process, after duties are paid equal to $1/m^2$. In total, there are 681 informal zones; in 152 (equal to 23,000 ha of land), technical and legal documentation are ready, while for 281 the process is under way. There are also some 98 zones or 168 ha that are occupied by group buildings (not classified as illegal settlements). ALUIZNI has logged a total of some 350,000 requests for legalization, of which some 80,000 were for multi-dwelling apartments and shops.

Source: Aldoni 2007.

Box 17: Legalization of illegal construction in informal settlements in Croatia and Armenia

The problem of illegal construction in Croatia is particularly significant in the coastal areas where it leads to informal settlement formation. In most cases, these are second homes or profit motivated developments that violate of planning and building permits. The problem escalated after 1995 when legalization regulations were revoked and possibilities of connection to infrastructure increased. For example, 9,000 illegal buildings were constructed on the island of Vir and another 1,800 in the coastal area of Rogoznica. The legacy of informal settlements in Croatia dates back to its socialist days. Regulations introduced in 1992 permitted legalization of all informal buildings (estimated at 100,000). Within three years, 35,000 building were legalized. The Directorate for Inspection Affairs within the Ministry of Environmental Protection and Physical Planning has taken measures to solve the problem of informal building. In the past three years, a total of 1,600 informally built buildings were demolished and another 4,000 were legalized. Prior to demolition, a detailed verification is carried out to check if the building is inhabited and/or if the residents also have other real estate. In such cases, demolitions are postponed. Legalization is integrated in the planning process (Tsenkova 2007).

In Armenia, new legislation encourages voluntary application by residents of unauthorized buildings and illegally occupied land to the State Real Property Cadastre Committee to formalize their ownership rights. The law sets certain fees based on the surface area of the construction and/or the plot of land. For the rights to be recognized, they must not conflict with urban development norms, nor limit other people's rights, and the property must be safe. The right of ownership is recognized if the land is acquired at its cadastral value. There is also a possibility of leasing the land/ property; leasing fees are also specified by law. The legalization process is expected to bring close to 320,000 illegal constructions into the formal housing market

Source: UNECE 2003.

Box 18: Legalizing informal settlements in the context of rapid urbanization in Turkey

Close to 10 million out of 44 million urban residents in Turkey today live in informal settlements, or *gecekondu*. The first attempt to legalize these developments dates back to the *Gecekondu* Act of 1966. With legal approval, *gecekondu* areas gained infrastructure as well as new roads and streets, but also subsequently grew in number and changed in character. Due to the lack of public land in the major cities, it became impossible for poor individuals to build their own *gecekondu*. Some of the new incomers had to become tenants of the *gecekondu* owners who had already constructed their second or third *gecekondu* to get rental income. The 1980s marked a period of increasing commodification, when soaring values of urban properties encouraged some *gecekondu* owners to pull their original houses down to build multi-storey ones either to rented or sell for profit. Aiming to legalize the existing stock and to solve the ownership problem of *gecekondu* settlements, 16 amnesty laws were adopted with accompanying improvement and development plans in the 1980s and early 1990s. This, however, has not prevented unregistered construction (close to 2 million just in Ankara, Istanbul and İzmir) and illegal urbanization in *gecekondu* settlements.

Source: Ozer et al. 2007.

2. Regularization and upgrading

Regularization and upgrading of informal settlements imply a more comprehensive intervention. For upgrading programmes to be effective, they must be integrated in the wider socio-economic context (e.g. a national strategy for poverty reduction). UN-Habitat highlights that "[The] problem of urban slums should be viewed within the broader context of the general failure of both welfare-oriented and market-based low-income housing policies and strategies in many (though not all) countries". Informal settlements should also be complemented by "clear and consistent policies for urban planning and management, as well as for low-income housing development" (UN-Habitat 2003).

Measures to prevent future formation of informal settlements must ensure that cost-effective housing development for low income groups is supported a sufficient and affordable supply of serviced land suitable for self-construction by the low-income groups. In situ upgrading is considered a more preferable solution to resettlement programmes. In recent years, there has been an important shift in implementing upgrading programmes. A new, more comprehensive approach gives greater emphasis on participation and partnerships and also on sustainable development as well as the need for simultaneous interventions with environmental, economic and social measures. Comprehensive and sustainable solutions for informal settlements must take account of both different local contexts and ways to mobilize the resources available at the local level. Solutions must be part of the broader urban and national development strategies supported by relevant institutional and legal frameworks.

Nowadays, solutions are hardly cut-and-dried, i.e. they are not simply legal or illegal, or formal or informal. The choice of approach to regularize informal settlements, e.g. legalization versus upgrading, will depend on the political will of the authorities, the lobbying and negotiating capacities of the residents and, last but not least, the location of the settlement itself – for example, its size and quality of housing. The practice of regularization and upgrading emphasizes the importance of intervention at three levels: the neighborhood (or informal settlement), the city and the metropolitan area or city region. While these are mostly planning interventions, the process usually incorporates land and real estate registration, plans for infrastructure provision, and social services (box 21).

At the neighborhood level, interaction with local authorities, planners, grass-roots community organizations, families and individuals delineates the immediate problems for residents vis-à-vis defining possible solutions. At the district/city level, urban planners and decision makers account for community dynamics and the impact of potential integration into the urban boundary in terms of transport and infrastructure requirements, costs and environmental implications. At the metropolitan/regional level, impacts and interaction within the urban agglomeration are considered, particularly in the case of large informal settlements, in order to make informed political and planning choices for the benefit of the city. Such a multi-level approach highlights inconsistencies and contradictions that may occur as well as the different political or financial priorities, thus redefining a more strategic urban planning approach to the complicated nature of the informal settlement integration. The process of actual integration is far more cumbersome, leaving much scope for conflicts between local governments, planners, investors and local residents.

Many NGOs and community-based organizations are using area-based urban development strategies to improve informal settlements. The strategy defines priorities, goals and objectives along with actions and a timeline for implementation. In essence, it is a community-level plan including a land-use plan, regulations for development, an infrastructure plan, a green-space plan and plans for location of social amenities (Carley 2001). The planning process is participatory in nature, bringing together stakeholders with a vested interest in the area. Urban planners often use a four-step process for informal settlement regularization and upgrading (Bolay 2006, World Bank 2001).

Step 1: Goal-setting. All stakeholders create realistic goals for the future, which include a vision of the informal settlement as a whole.

Step 2: Action. The action plan includes: (a) provision of communal and social infrastructure; and (b) provisions for interdepartmental coordination and management. It is important that progress is noticeable. If informal residents see action, they will realize that their opinions are valuable and that positive and sustainable change is possible. Residents need to feel that improving their community is an investment in their future and the future of their children.

Step 3: Community participation and capacity-building. It is extremely important to have a forum where all stakeholders can come together to express concerns and optimism about the future of informal housing settlements. Community-based actions (as in the cases of the Russian Federation and Gorica, Bosnia and Herzegovina; see boxes 18 and 19) and consensus on the most important measures to be implemented makes residents involved and responsible for change. At the settlement level, residents need to take initiative, ownership and responsibility as well as contribute financially.

Box 19: Bringing citizens' voices into formal urban decision-making

To ensure that deprived palaces and residents are included into the formal system of housing and utility management and maintenance, it is important to support the development of housing movements and to build on these bottom-up initiatives.

In response to "unfair" legal provisions to eliminate degrading housing and utilities, a number of housing movements have been established recently in the Russian Federation. Such bottom-up organizations can be found in about 40 Russian regions. People claim respect for their constitutional housing rights and for better control over the housing and utility reform and decision-making processes that directly affect their lives. They want the State to recognize the equal status of community-based organizations to manage multi-family houses or set clear rules to stimulate other forms of housing management. Experts estimate that in the future such housing movements may represent a real challenge for authorities, who will need to find ways to engage in dialogue with citizens. The authorities will need to build on these bottom-up initiatives if they want to establish effective policies. Today, neither authorities nor citizens have the capacity for productive discussions. Main obstacles are lack of trust in the State apparatus and appointed officials, lack of a tradition of self-organizing reinforced by market individualism and conflicts of interest between homeowners with different socio-economic status. It has been argued that building collective responsibilities should be stimulated. Recently, an organization called "the Housing Strategy" has been set up to support citizens and small and medium businesses in the housing and utility services sector. The organization intends to enhance the professionalism of resident groups and small and medium businesses to deal with housing and utility issues, thus creating a competitive environment for the provision of housing and utility services.

Other important issues of debate in the Russian Federation at the moment include the need to develop a non-for-profit housing sector to allow low-income groups to access decent housing at an affordable rent. The development of such housing stock is also crucial for addressing the problem of resettlement from unsafe housing.

Box 20: Regularization of the Gorica Settlement in Bosnia and Herzegovina

The Gorica Roma settlement of approximately 60 households, located in Sarajevo, occupies a parcel of land owned partly by a State-owned enterprise and partly by the Municipality. After the 1996 war, displaced families returned to Gorica and reconstructed their homes even though the threat of eviction from the area, designated for a park, was still imminent. In 2000, an association of Gorica residents mobilized several international organizations, including the Organization for Security and Co-operation in Europe, the Office of the United Nations High Commissioner for Human Rights and Office of the United Nations High Commissioner for Refugees, as well as donor organizations, to resolve its housing situation once and for all. The association pressed its case with all competent municipal departments through letters, meetings and public protests. A regularization process was initiated including re-zoning for residential uses, compensation of the State enterprise by the municipality and transfer of ownership to Roma residents in 2002. Since the municipality was concerned with the issue of adequacy of housing, it sought assurances from the donors that adequate housing would be provided. Reconstruction in Gorica started in the spring of 2002 under the auspices of World Vision. The Gorica experience highlights several lessons that are relevant to other prospective regularization processes:

Roma communities must provide the impetus for regularization. The early and sustained engagement of the Gorica Roma community in the effort to resolve their insecure housing situation was a key factor in achieving the regularization of their settlement. Gorica benefited from good local leadership that promoted solidarity among residents and represented their interests in an open and effective way;

- Partnerships are instrumental in overcoming the legal, political and financial challenges involved in regularizations. The Roma community of Gorica cultivated good working relationships with local government, civil society and international organizations.

- Regularizations require inventive solutions such as rezoning, compensation and reassurances for housing improvements and follow up investment.

- Regularizations require long term commitment. It took 15 years from the first expropriations to the final step to fully secure the tenure of the residents of Gorica.

Source: OSCE 2006.

Step 4: Accountability processes. These are necessary to report results and make residents and local government accountable for change. Part of the accountability process is to ensure that information is shared with all stakeholders and that no one hoards information; this can be mitigated through active support from major stakeholders. Accountability also involves continuing policy revision to adapt to the changing needs of communities, from response and feedback, integrated into urban planning strategies for informal housing settlements.

Building and maintaining infrastructure and public amenities are major steps in formalizing and upgrading informal settlements. Once an informal housing settlement is deemed fit to stay, it is essential to create joint partnerships to help pay the costs of upgrading (box 21). It is important for residents to pay a minimal cost for infrastructure and amenities, which helps create an appreciation for services. It is desirable for residents to monitor settlement growth if others are trying to illegally acquire services. One way of improving infrastructure is to collect fees from those using the infrastructure, with the proviso that services are guaranteed.

Governments need to develop an infrastructure fee structure based on income, a method of encouraging residents to contribute that assures them that infrastructure access will be affordable. In addition, Governments need to allocate funds in their capital budget to address the lack of infrastructure, which creates multiple disadvantages for the residents in informal housing settlements. Investment in infrastructure development often includes the following steps:

- Planning the location of current and future sewage lines
- Making sure everyone has access to clean water
- Determining suitable landfill and solid waste location centres
- Developing an appropriate road network

Government should provide equal access to basic infrastructure since this is fundamental to delivering equal and affordable access to housing. Citizens should contribute to the costs whenever feasible. Investment in the city-wide infrastructure is a precondition for successful and affordable upgrading of deprived neighbourhoods (or settlements), as the lack of such provision can reinforce the exclusion of the urban poor and prevent their access to affordable housing (UN-Habitat 2003). Investment in city-wide infrastructure by the public sector is a significant part of making housing affordable for the poor in upgraded informal settlements, as is providing a supportive environment for the informal enterprises established by the poor residents. Future low-income housing and upgrading policies for informal settlements therefore need to pay greater attention to the financing of city-wide infrastructure development.

A comprehensive approach to upgrading informal settlements has not proved an easy task. The various and complex issues connected with informal settlements are often handled separately dealt by different sectors and are often fragmented among different levels of government. Strategic approaches that can achieve long-term solutions are lacking at the national level. Tighter integration is needed between the community and the regional and national authorities, as well as with other key stakeholders. There is still too much emphasis placed on physical elements and other technical issues in upgrading programmes, which come at the expense of needed focus on social issues. The brooader framework recognizing the need to support livelihood based on basic human rights has still to be developed.

Several successful practices from the case studies can be highlighted. Bottom-up initiatives with an active community participation in decision-making and management of the transformation of informal settlements have been central to the successful implementation of the upgrading projects. The cooperation of different key players at the beginning of the projects and the establishment of partnerships have been a powerful instrument. Significant contribution has been made through innovative ways such as zoning and compensation; these stimulated housing improvements and further investments. A crucial issue for the implementation of the projects in a sustainable way has been the emphasis on a long term commitment with clear objectives. The important contribution has been made by the local players and Governments participating in the decision-making and management of issues related to current and future local needs.

Box 21: Challenges in legalizing and upgrading of informal settlements in Greece

Illegal construction in Greece, resulting in informal settlements, dates back to the 1950s. The reasons are complicated and have changed through the years. Informal settlements now occur in industrial zones, urban fringe areas and in rural areas, including attractive vacation areas. Several attempts have been made to minimize the problem either by applying procedures aiming at informal settlements' integration into a city plan with a simultaneous provision of urban planning improvements (e.g. the Laws of 1977 and 1983), in parallel with tough penalties (e.g. the Law of 2003), or locally through extensions of the existing urban plans, in some cases resettlement. Nevertheless, none of the applied procedures have proven adequate to stop the creation of new informal construction. Some projects have been successful, but most have proven to be costly and time-consuming due to the lack of modern, national tools (e.g. a national cadastre and other necessary spatial information infrastructure) and poor coordination between the various land-related agencies involved in development and permitting procedures.

The real size of the problem is difficult to estimate due to a lack of information. In fact, all projects for new urban land refer to areas with existing unplanned developments. As mentioned above, these include both legal and illegal construction, since construction in areas without a detailed city plan is permitted in Greece. Many regularization and upgrading projects have been carried out in Greece since 1982, as "urban regeneration projects".

Recent estimates by the Hellenic Chamber of Commerce show that informal settlements in Greece contain as many as 1,000,000 residences (or 15 per cent of the total). The majority are concentrated in 7 prefectures (out of a total of 13). The "new generation" of informal buildings consists of constructions of one or two storeys on land parcels of 1,000–1,500 m². Studies indicate that some 93,000 legal and 31,000 informal residences are constructed annually, equivalent to a small town. The biggest problem exists is the Attica region, comprising the greater metropolitan area of Athens and its rapid urbanization. A massive cadastral project under way is expected to provide useful documentation on the current situation with orthophoto maps and a linking of parcels with updated legal rights. A coordination of these data with urban regeneration/upgrading projects is also expected

Sources: Potsiou and Ioannidis 2006, Potsiou and Muller 2007, Potsiou and Dimitriadi 2008.

Box 22: Legalization and upgrading of borgate in Rome

Rome had 750,000 illegally constructed rooms in 1977 or 20 per cent of city's total stock, mostly located at the periphery of the city. Abusivismo is illegally constructed housing, usually in violation of land-use and building regulations. Baracche (shacks) and borgate (shanty towns) are part of abusivismo, as is illegal housing built by the comparatively well-off. The Italian Senate approved the Condono Edilizio to legalize unauthorized housing from 1983 to 1985, since the problem was significant not just in Rome but also in other large Italian cities. Borgate is the term for illegal settlements in the urban periphery of Rome but within the city limits. These settlements were overcrowded, lacked roads, water, sewage and electricity. When the leftist majority municipal government accepted responsibility for the borgate, they were integrated into the General Regulatory Plan in the early 1980s, and thus legally incorporated into the city of Rome. This was a stimulus for systematic improvement of primary infrastructure and public services. Plans for public transport, schools and cultural centres were developed; a speeding-up of the process of bringing illegal buildings into code. The costs were partly covered by a special tax the residents had to pay to legalize their property. At the time of legalization, some borgate had more than 50,000 inhabitants. Companies settled there due to their favourable location, and the links with the centre intensified. The ex-post facto provision of technical infrastructure was undoubtedly more expensive than planned development, but it required less public investment than solutions in line with traditional urban planning practices, namely social housing for poor immigrants. The time required to integrate poor migrants into the urban system is longer than budgetary cycles or legislative periods. It took two generations to transform the marginalized borgate in Rome into modern suburbs. The settlers had to accumulate a certain level of wealth, initially based mainly on homeownership. Then they needed to be integrated into the urban economy. In the final stage, they could adapt their norms and ways of life to modern urban standards.

Source: Kreibich 2000.

3. Resettlement and reallocation: an issue for public housing

One possible solution to informal settlement problems has been implemented in different countries across the UNECE region: resettlement in social housing or some form of subsidized formal housing developments. In most cases, resettlement targets poor residents of informal settlements or vulnerable groups such as Roma, refugees and IDPs. This is an expensive solution and it is not surprising that its implementation is limited. However, the modest application of this approach may also be related to the underdeveloped institution of public housing as a complementary option to the private housing choices. Policies for public housing, if appropriately designed, can be a good way to address the housing choices of low-income groups.

In certain countries with a strong tradition of public/municipal housing and where the State – or the private companies close to the State – have significant presence in the housing and land market, resettlement and reallocation are favored practices in urban renewal and regeneration of central urban areas that have problems of overcrowding and neighborhood deprivation. Governments are actively involved in the housing market through partnerships with developers. In general, the response is the demolition of dilapidated housing and the resettlement of low-income groups to the peripheral areas of a city either in private (in cases where a private developer is responsible) or in municipally owned estates. The allocation of different income-groups within different areas of a city becomes a solution to their different housing problems. The central areas then become available for higher-income groups. Such practices address housing problems of certain social groups, but create problems of a different sort – social segregation and inequality are further reinforced by spatially neutral responses to housing problems. Therefore, resettlement and allocation in public housing should take into consideration the possible negative implications of social segregation. These are important in case of overcrowded, substandard or deprived neighborhoods in inner cities, where existing housing stock cannot be preserved and upgrading cannot be facilitated.

In other countries, there is no general model for social housing to support the difficult task of integrating large groups of migrants, often poor, into existing cities. Macro determinants and local settings vary to such a degree that specific solutions are required (Bruto da Costa and Baptista 2001, UN-HABITAT 2003). It seems, however, that the local administrative and political systems are rarely able to develop and implement appropriate concepts and strategies. Notwithstanding these challenges, two examples from Portugal and Spain illustrate potential solutions to resettlement (see boxes 22 and 23).

The importance of effective social policies and programmes that provide access to equal, safe and affordable housing for informal residents, while widely recognized, are in many cases beyond the financial and institutional capacities of central and local governments, particularly in countries affected by war and refugee crises. Many of the global commitments of United Nations declarations, the European Charter and national plans seek to achieve well-functioning social housing policies, are implemented with effective programmes to help those who need support. In reality, efforts to reduce social inequality, to ensure security and social cohesion and to provide safe housing in many countries where informal settlements are an enduring element of growing cities, have achieved modest results. Policies to help IDPs, refugees and other socially vulnerable groups are vital to their integration in society, but in some transition countries the solution is severely constrained by the emerging vicious circle in the urban economy. Local governments often have limited investment capacity, weak revenue bases and increased dependence on central government transfers. Meanwhile, they are faced with growing responsibilities and managerial tasks, including effective planning and land management, development control and increased demands for basic services.

With concentrations of poor and disadvantaged residents in precarious housing conditions, some local governments are obviously unable to break the circle which affects not only the prospects of individual cities and their residents, but ultimately national economies as well. It comes as no surprise that in the context of transition, most of the solutions to poverty and informal settlement proliferation are ad hoc, small-scale crisis management interventions.

The limited success of public housing programmes may also be attributed to a number of factors. Economic growth has been given higher priority over social issues due to strong beliefs in market efficiency and the trickle-down effect. Aspects of the problem may be scepticism in the political discourse on social housing and the low esteem of representations in the media. There is also insufficient knowledge about the centrality of the housing sector to social development and economic growth.

Given limited governmental resources and capacity, the complex reality of the housing question cannot be resolved by relying solely on strict rules, top-down reactive strategies and technical knowledge, nor can it be resolved by simply improving homes per se. It is necessary to find creative approaches that deal with the problem in a larger sense, improving conditions of living and reviving communities. There is a need to change ineffective models of public housing provision. Governments must recognize their role in the contemporary market context: they must provide diversity and flexibility in public housing choices. An enabling environment should be created to ensure that housing via the private housing market also allows equal and affordable access for all income groups.

It is essential that the resettlement and allocation approach to informal settlements is integrated with effective poverty-reduction strategies that recognize basic human rights, i.e. which ensure social stability, create a sense of place and hope for the marginalized groups and give a vision and promise for the future. Poverty reduction strategies, however, must recognize the wider context in which informal settlements operate. Housing is a key dimension of social inequality. Luxurious housing enclaves for the rich strata of population become landmarks to the new urban lifestyle, whereas other areas with dilapidated, rundown or other substandard housing are continually neglected.

There have been limited examples in which the social housing supply for low-income groups really has achieved wider social objectives. The housing problem demands novel and innovative solutions Developed countries such as France, the Netherlands and the United Kingdom are very much concerned with finding a feasible solution to the housing problem. The failure of the public sector to create decent housing prospects for low-income people has served to reinforce social inequalities and created stigmatized places of blight and distress with high rates of unemployment and concentration of people depending on State support.

Currently, the housing sector can be described as pro-homeownership and as structured by inequality of supply and demand. Housing for high- and very high-income groups assumes a much larger share of residential construction at the same time that housing demand is dominated by the consumption preferences of high-income groups. Some Governments have introduced targeting programmes to house the most disadvantaged groups. While these housing choices are limited to certain places and target poor people, the private housing market lacks affordability. Effective functioning of the social housing sector is severely curtailed by its targeting strategies, as it concentrates people who have limited ability to pay back the housing costs.

There are examples of recent urban strategies to break the vicious circle of deprivation and marginalization. One such policy (in the United Kingdom) focuses on addressing the stigmatization of social housing by reshaping its image. Achieving a social mix has become a key concept to shape policy interventions in deprived neighbourhoods. Housing solutions are also driven by a number of "socially responsible" public-private partnerships and appropriate supporting legal frameworks also have to be established. If social housing is to contribute to broader social objectives and sustainable development, this will require innovative means to supply housing that meets low-income groups' needs as well as effective management decisions regarding the maintenance of social housing stock. Such decisions must be supported by new financial and legal instruments.

Furthermore, public housing should not be considered as a separate system to satisfy the needs of low-income groups, but must be integrated into a unified residential market. Creating a housing system that provides fair, affordable and diverse choices for low-income groups requires a new vision and long-term national and local strategies. There is also a need to tap the social housing sector's potential to contribute to sustainable development. Housing strategies should be based on a human right approach, one that is based on an understanding of shelter's myriad functions, inter alia, security, family life, a base for work and leisure, and a place to escape from the problems of the outside world.

Box 23: Special rehousing programme in the Lisbon and Porto metropolitan areas

More than 130,000 families living in shanty towns in the metropolitan areas of Lisbon and Porto have (or will have) access to adequate housing, in some cases after living in shanty towns for generations.[10] The Special Rehousing Programme, or Programa Especial de Realojamento (PER), launched in 1993, was expected to eliminate the shanty towns in the 27 participating municipalities by 2001. It was the manifestation of an ideological slogan that emerged from the 1974 Revolution: "Houses yes, barracks no!" Social housing, mostly in high-density housing estates in the Lisbon and Porto metropolitan areas, has become the new home of more than 94,000 families. PER is still 30 per cent short of its original target and its time frame has been extended. The programme operates with the extensive support of the central government, which covers 40 per cent of the costs. Another 40 per cent is assumed by municipalities through soft loans that totaled €1,280 million at the end of 2006. The remaining 20 per cent is municipal in-kind contributions through land and infrastructure. The housing is built by private firms under contractual arrangement at fixed prices regulated by the State. In Lisbon, housing provided through PER has added close to 30 per cent to the social housing stock (8,700 apartments). This recent growth as a result of the reallocation initiatives (by PER and its predecessor) has posed new challenges to these new urban territories' management. The need for the integrated management of the public housing stock (new and old), with different sets of urban, social and economic problems being identified, calls for the gradual involvement of the different public and private actors within a system of organized

partnership. The PER experience has seen the emergence of some successful initiatives in this domain, and one may expect improvement towards the more efficient management of the new housing estates in response to the changing needs of the residents.

Source: Tsenkova, interview data, Lisbon 2007.

---

[10] The number of residents covered by PER in the metropolitan area of Lisbon is 115,641, or 34,498 families. In the metropolitan area of Porto, eligible residents numbered 39, 776 (or 14,269 families).

Box 24: Resettlement of *chabolistas* in Madrid

In the late 1980s, more than 100,000 people lived in *chabolas*, illegal shacks and temporary houses. These were mostly migrants from rural Extremadura and Andalusia, who settled on small plots not zoned for housing and built shacks without permits. Some of these neighborhoods in the South of Madrid were fairly large (e.g. Palomeras had 28,000 residents living in 7,600 *chabolas*). Most were not serviced, with water trucked in. A radical call for "adequate housing here and now" resulted in the largest operation of urban renewal in Madrid's history. The project was implemented with extensive public participation. Due to the engagement of community groups, innovative solutions came about. The former *chabolistas* could choose if they wanted to rent or buy their new flats; the majority preferred the model of social housing. They accepted living in multi-storey blocks and having their flats assigned at random. When they had arrived at the point where they could influence the type of their new housing and the structure of their future neighborhoods, they did not hesitate to opt for "modern housing". Representatives of the neighborhood organizations oversaw the construction process. After they had moved into their new flats, the neighborhood groups started to call for improved social services (e.g. nurseries and primary schools, sporting grounds, a social centre and a club for senior citizens). The organizations managed to achieve housing and planning standards that the Government would have never granted the *chabolistas* without the latter's proactive participation. After almost 14 years, the high-rise housing estates of the *gran operación* are still areas with social problems and conflicts, but from the perspectives of urban planning and neighborhood management they are quite stable.

Sources: Heitkamp 2000 and Kreibich 2000.

4. Alternative housing systems for informal settlements

The choice of resettlement to social housing is being substantially curtailed by the diminishing role of government. Other alternative options have been backed by policymakers dealing with informal settlements. A greater focus has been placed on the creating an enabling environment, greater involvement of communities in decision-making processes and mobilizing their resources for low-cost, self-help housing construction. Governments have promoted alternative housing finance systems that allow access to credit for the urban poor and disadvantaged. These small credits, often micro-loans, encourage the improvement of informal housing and assist with legalization costs. If an informal settlement is deemed fit for occupancy, local governments should work with national bodies and civil society to promote affordable finance tools that can be accessed by residents. This will encourage the development of "suitable" settlements and make funds available for housing improvements. It would be a mutually beneficial situation for residents and local governments. Lending providers and local governments can justify the expense as an initial investment having the impact of long-term investment. Upgrading in this way seems to be the least expensive approach for government to deal with urban poverty.

However, the "minimal State" approach has been widely criticized. For sustainable solutions to be good practice examples, both the "humanistic" and "authoritarian" models are essential and should complement each other (Werlin 1999). The humanistic approach has been a response to the limitations of top-down decision-making and of Governments in terms of adequate resources and capacity. This model is based on the belief that people and communities have a great potential for self-organization, self-mobilization and management of their resources "from below'. For the transformation of informal settlements to be successful, it is necessary for people and communities to actively participate and influence the ways in which their needs and future opportunities are addressed. This will prevent the multiple disadvantages they encounter. However, it has also been argued that for such a people-based approach to work and be sufficiently organized, it must still be connected to and guided by administration at higher levels. In some countries with a tradition of a "strong" State, it may take more time for people and Governments to create an enabling environment for self-organization and active participation, and thus some oversight is important. Furthermore, a strong tendency towards individualistic consumption has already had negative implications for mutual support and collective action. Such a negative tendency is even stronger in some transition countries where collective action and egalitarianism were driving ideologies in the past. Specific seminars and educational courses may help people improve their knowledge and understanding of such tools and policies.

The market is one of the desirable solutions to the housing question; ideally, it can offer flexibility and a variety of housing choices of good quality. However, such benefits are not guaranteed to be distributed fairly between people and places. To deal with unsystematic and disordered urban development, appropriate policies must be applied and enabling environments for collective action must be created. Uncontrolled residential development may further reinforce the problems of deprivation and the exclusion of informal settlements. Mobilizing local practices as part of the solution to informal settlements is a field for further exploration and learning.

The interest in policy based on local knowledge is in line with the model proposed recently by UN-Habitat, which establishes linkages between local and national processes and between the poor and the State. This model looks at how local skills and resources can be efficiently integrated into the broader policy framework and decision-making processes, and may offer a powerful tool to achieve sustainable communities. In this way, "the risk of instrumentalization, politicization and polarization which constitute a continuous threat to the accountability of poverty reduction programmes" can be avoided because the model "recognizes the fundamental right of adequate shelter, and grants to the poor an equal share of political participation, satisfaction of habitat needs and resource investment in the fields of education, capacity development, services, infrastructure, income and labour generation" (UN-Habitat, Social Production of Habitat as a viable alternative, 2003). This model recognizes both key actors: citizens and the public authorities. Future development, if to be shaped by this innovative concept, must simultaneously work on four fronts: (a) shelter; (b) responsible citizenship; (c) productive environments; and (d) sustainable urban development. The model emphasizes "collective human rights, socialized responsibilities and accountability", and is thus fundamentally different from market-based individualistic approaches.

5. Addressing the challenge of substandard inner-city housing: urban renewal and regeneration strategies

A number of countries in the UNECE region are addressing the need for affordable and adequate housing through area-based urban renewal and regeneration programmes. While these programmes do not necessarily target informal settlements, they do aim to improve substandard housing. Illegality in this case is manifested in overcrowded conditions, sublets, and in more general terms, social exclusion. Commitment at the national level, particularly in Western Europe, has created a supportive framework for local action (Kleinhans et al 2007). Many local authorities have managed to create coalitions and partnerships to increase the affordable housing supply and to assist vulnerable groups through urban regeneration projects (Tsenkova 2004). Local governments, working in partnership with private developers as well as non-profit housing providers and community groups, have experimented with inner-city regeneration, including brownfield and waterfront redevelopment schemes. The search for effective strategies for urban regeneration – to create a social mix, increase the supply of affordable housing and facilitate investment and improvement of existing infrastructure – has promoted new models (Kleinhans et al. 2007). Urban regeneration has challenged social housing providers to develop a new repertoire of instruments that deal simultaneously with physical deprivation and social exclusion in local communities.

Urban renewal programmes exist in most European cities with an aging housing stock and substandard housing in inner-city areas. Barcelona, Copenhagen, Lisbon, Manchester and Vienna are well known for their successful "soft-renewal" practices and strategic approaches underlying social, economic, cultural, and environmental factors. Recent urban renewal programmes have placed particular emphasis on public-private partnerships as the delivery mechanism, as well as on public involvement and participation in defining priorities for given area or neighbourhood. Attempts are being made to reduce displacement as well as to avoid forced change of ownership, social segregation and gentrification (Atkinson 2000, Donner 2000).

The European Union also recognizes that cities are the engines of innovation and economic growth, but they are also frequently the locations of serious problems, inter alia inner-city decline, housing deprivation, unemployment, physical decay and social exclusion. The ability of local communities to address these problems through planning and policy intervention centred on urban renewal is essential for the long-term performance of cities (where 80 per cent of the people in the EU live and work). In this context, EU support for urban policy implementation is essential. The URBAN I Community Initiative, launched in the period 1994–1999 with €900 million, comprised 118 programmes benefiting nearly 3 million inhabitants. It targeted poor inner-city and peripheral urban areas, mostly through physical and environmental regeneration, entrepreneurship and social inclusion. The URBAN II initiative, which covered the period 2000–2006, built on the integrated approach to urban regeneration and was designed to promote economic and social regeneration in small- and medium-sized towns and declining areas in major conurbations. The 70 programmes included in URBAN II received a total European Regional Development Fund (ERDF) contribution of €728 million. This was allocated to 175 cities in the EU. Through co-financing mechanisms, this contribution has actually enabled a total investment of €1.6 billion focused on social inclusion, and physical and environmental improvement (Turró et al. 2007).

The role of cities for contemporary global economic, technological and cultural processes has been significant. Cities have become recognized as places concentrating the assets essential to support the growth of the national economy as well as social development. They are thus necessary to succeed in global competition. Deprivation and wealth accumulated unevenly within different urban neighbourhoods (or informal settlements) are the examples of uneven redistribution of these important assets.

The multiple problems of deprived neighbourhood require an innovative comprehensive approach based on the comprehension that it is a dialectical relationship between social and physical processes that contribute to such deprivation. Social structures affect physical environment of neighbourhoods and visa versa. Social inequality and exclusion are not the only forces responsible for precarious living conditions in certain neighbourhoods; such places are also excluded from the wider urban structure and planning strategies as well as from mainstream economic, political and social development.

The growing recognition of these simultaneous processes has stimulated the emergence of new urban renewal strategies that focus on place-based action (e.g. the importance of interventions at a certain spatial level) and that emphasize public participation (e.g. empowering communities and allowing their stake in the urban renewal). Tackling social exclusion through area-based programmes is one solution, as programmes can be highly relevant in certain contexts but not in others. They are mostly suitable for areas in which multiple problems of deprivation have become spatially concentrated. In other cases, where there is no such "neighborhood effect", and other policies may be more relevant (e.g. subsidies, different forms of social support).

Nevertheless, some countries have been very progressive in exploring new approaches to urban renewal. The United Kingdom has been one of the leaders in establishing effective strategies for places and people. The Government has recently launched a National Strategy for Neighbourhood Renewal to address deprived neighbourhoods in an integrated way, simultaneous focusing on social, economic and environmental issues at the neighbourhood level. The Strategy is also designed to ensure that the solutions are coordinated across different sectors at different levels of government, and that all relevant voices are included and have a stake. In particular, there is a close linkage between urban renewal programmes and national shelter strategies. In this way, housing assumes a pivotal role in promoting the objective of a social mix (i.e. the integration of the high-income and low-income groups in the same neighborhood). There is also a shift towards adopting people-focused regeneration strategies rather than simply on improving physical structures. (This is sometimes defined as "soft" regeneration strategies versus "bricks and mortar'). "Bricks-and-mortar" interventions are partial responses and need to be complemented by "soft" strategies aiming to change lives and prospects for the people in deprived areas. People- or community-based initiatives are now being explored to support policymaking and to achieve better outcomes for interventions in deprived neighbourhoods. Social capital is becoming a new paradigm for urban renewal programmes.

In the context of Netherlands, urban renewal strategies can also be characterized as an area-based approach. The key concepts are integrated, area-based and decentralized interventions. The approach addresses two major problems: "social exclusion problems" and "integration". The integration strategy is based on three major pillars: physical, economic and social. To tackle social exclusion, the importance of social cohesion and the promotion of social mix is emphasized. Special free funds to support physical, economic and social solutions are available. One persistent problem, however, is that issues are still dealt with separately within these funds, and this tends to hamper overall integration. Moreover, there has been only a modest achievement of a social mix. Too much weight is still given to physical problems. Dilapidated housing stocks have often been replaced by new high-quality housing, and thus upgrading is being achieved at the expense of low-income groups.

Most recent policies give greater initial attention to neighborhood quality and the community and only then to physical restructuring. There have been some recommendations to develop policies "that lead to social mobility, investment in education, offering the opportunity to realize small steps on the housing ladder and refraining from physical interventions" (Masterd and Ostendorf 2008). An important finding has been the contradiction between, on one hand, a political discourse on deprived neighborhoods as highly segregated places and, on the other, the reality of vibrant and dynamic places with a mixture of different cultures (ibid.). It is rather luxurious housing enclaves that segregate and depart from the active urban life more precipitously, and which thus should be subjected to change as well.

Box 25: Dutch urban regeneration: focus on deprived neighborhoods

The national Big Cities Policy is helping the four largest cities in the Netherlands to respond to the problems of high unemployment, crime, polarization and growing spatial concentrations of low-income households and ethnic minority groups, as well as the physical problems often found in social housing. The Big Cities Policy rests on three pillars: (a) the economy and employment; (b) the physical infrastructure; and (c) the social infrastructure. Funding is used in an integrated manner to improve the quality of urban space, to create more jobs and to eliminate social exclusion in neighborhoods. This area-based approach focuses on deprived neighborhoods and contributes to social cohesion through measures implemented by residents, government bodies (e.g. local authorities, police and social welfare organizations), housing associations and local employers.

Source: Van Kempen 2000.

In Amsterdam, where more than half of the housing is social, non-profit housing associations own 205.000 social rental dwellings. While these are distributed across the city in every district, a fair number are concentrated in post-war neighborhoods such as the Western Garden Cities and the south-east. Over time, although the housing is in good condition, these areas have become less desirable places to live, with social exclusion and poverty manifested in a number of ways. The new wave of government investment leverages contributions from the housing associations and aims at creating a social mix of rental and owner-occupied housing. Less popular high-rise apartments in the target neighborhoods are being demolished and replaced by medium-density dwellings often in mixed ownership neighborhood blocks. Housing allowances continue to support low-income households, and displacement is being managed through reallocation programmes by housing associations active in the neighborhoods.

Source: Tsenkova, interview data, October 2007.

Box 26: Vienna's urban renewal programme

In Vienna, where half of the housing stock is social housing, subsidies are an important aspect of the city's urban renewal programme. The amount of subsidies granted for a particular project are dependent on the standard of the existing building, but can be up to 90 per cent of total construction costs. This also includes an allowance for low-income households to reduce short-term costs involved with renovations (problems with allowance programmes). The renewal is followed by a controlled and limited rent increase for 15 years to cover any loans required. Any type of building is eligible for a renewal (construction) subsidy, including private rentals or owner-occupied units.

One such example is Gasometer City, a brownfield redevelopment around four large gas tanks built in 1899, but had not been used since 1986. Vienna decided this would be a project to spearhead development in this previously industrial area. The new multifunctional area with 620 units of subsidized housing, 250 student hostel units, 47,100 m² of commercial space, offices and a theatre has become the catalyst for the redevelopment of the whole neighbourhood.

Source: www.wien.at.

CHAPTER 5

Policy principles and guidelines

In general, the problems of informal settlements in countries in transition have not been systematically addressed and responsibilities remain fragmented. Informal settlements and residents have often been neglected in the broader urban and social development practices. Some communities in informal settlements have opted for self-organization, these initiatives being often backed up by the media, local governments, international organizations and NGOs. While these cases may be limited, the process of self-organization has had many positive outcomes. Currently, however, there is a global call for urgent yet sustainable interventions for informal settlements. Governments are translating relevant global strategies into specific national contexts. Higher-level government is increasingly seen as a key enabler of change with respect to informal settlements. There is also a commitment to ensure equal access to basic human rights as well as fairness in wealth redistribution and poverty reduction. Public-private partnerships are often at the centre of decision-making. A strong tendency towards mobilizing local skills and knowledge can also be noted.

Based on findings from case studies and in-depth discussions with a group of experts on informal settlements in UNECE member States, the present study proposes a framework to guide future policy interventions. The recommendations presented here are based on this policy framework. Figure 9 presents a simplified version of the framework, which embraces the complexity of the informal settlements as a multileveled socio-spatial formation requiring a comprehensive approach, namely a sustainable combination of policy solutions that take into account the different spatialities (socio-spatial arrangements) affecting living standards in informal settlements. The spider graph (i.e. framework) does not try to portray exactly the informal settlements reality, but rather aims to stimulate debate about the different dimensions of the informal settlements habitat and the design of sustainable policy interventions. The framework tries to integrate the perspective of the United Nations

Millennium Development Goals, namely a recognition of the connection of material dispossession of people to socio-spatial polarization (e.g. the emergence of deprived areas and communities on the one hand, and luxurious housing enclaves for the wealthiest social groups on the other). The framework is also relevant for other cases in which poverty (e.g. lack of economic assets) may not be an issue for residents of informal settlements, but where it is rather a lack of other assets (e.g. adequate regulations/institutions) that entraps the residents. These various disparities all put sustainable urban development at risk.

Figure 9: Informal settlement diagram

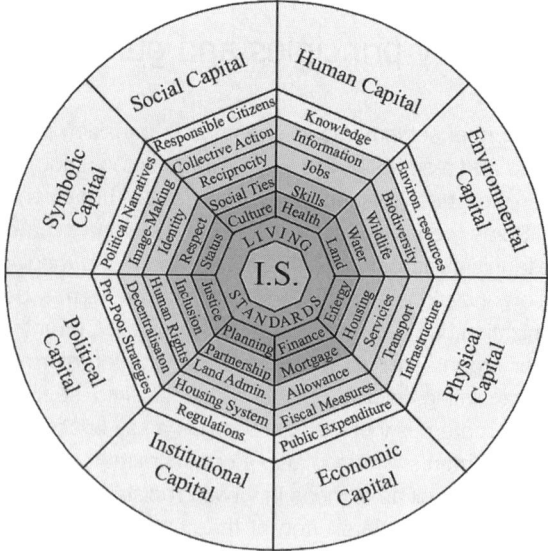

A broad spectrum of urban development projects have been undertaken in the last 20 years (e.g. in Greece, Italy, Portugal and Spain). As mentioned earlier, solutions range from legalization and regularization to providing essential social and physical infrastructure to resettlement programmes in social housing to inclusion in formal urban planning. Evidence has shown that it is only through adopting comprehensive, integrated solutions that better outcomes for informal settlement interventions can be achieved. Successful responses should be based on acknowledging varied forces behind different types of informal settlements and the need to apply a range of policy tools (e.g. social, economic, spatial planning) simultaneously. For such integrations to be effective, they must be framed by long-term strategies aimed at achieving wider societal goals, which in turn are based on the principles of sustainability and social fairness. Equal, affordable and safe access to the basic human rights of land and shelter are preconditions for development of sustainable places and communities.

A number of problems have prevented existing informal settlement programmes from achieving successful outcomes. Insufficient financial and human resources, burdensome regulatory rules, unclear administrative procedures and unrealistic standards are some of the major barriers. In some cases, responses have been reactive and hostile rather than comprehensive, strategic and proactive. The failure of many programmes can be attributed to a misunderstanding of the deeper causes underlying informal settlement formations, e.g. social inequality, uneven distribution of wealth or poor access to funding mechanisms and a limited application of such policy tools as integrated land management and spatial planning. Responses to the housing question often remain very technical and the development of the housing sector has not been given a priority it deserves within the context of national economic and social development. The proper coordination ofn housing policy and other policies has yet to be achieved. In addition, the belief in the market as a "one-size-fits-all" solution often further marginalizes alternative developments and reinforces the problems of informal settlements.

The following lessons for policy consideration can be drawn from the existing experiences. It is important to consider a number of important initiatives when translating the informal settlements agenda into local contexts. Better outcomes have been possible thanks to:

a. Changes in policymaking, including a move towards a strategic vision, and planning for short-term, medium and long-term solutions;

b. Creation of an effective governance framework that comprises key actors from different fields and empowers voices of marginalized groups;

c. Establishment of a platform for dialogue between key actors as well as of effective public-private partnerships;

d. Willingness to draw on existing practices and learn from other experiences to support the policy process, and an eagerness for continuous learning and knowledge-sharing;

e. A new commitment to fighting social inequality and establishing social justice;

f. Thorough analysis of the major causes affecting residents" living conditions;

g. Establishment of efficient linkages between major policy fields, e.g. housing, land management and spatial planning;

h. Development of urban strategies that focus on the settlement level, but take account of the importance of informal settlements' connection to broader social, economic, environmental and urban development processes.

Based on this study, the following key policy principles and guidelines are proposed to guide informal settlement interventions. Although not all-encompassing, these are intended to provide a framework for policymakers by identifying the main areas and actions for successful interventions.

PRINCIPLE 1

There is no "one-size-fits-all" solution to address the problems of informal settlements. The choice of policy tools should be comprehensive and consider the specific socio-cultural context.

Rationale:

Processes behind the formation of informal settlement are embedded in particular national contexts. It is necessary to remember that what works well in one context may fail in another. Policy responses to informal settlements need to be based on a comprehensive analysis of the underlying causes and consequences of informal settlements in the particular context of the country/territory in question.

It is also extremely important that policymaking reflect an understanding of the multiple problems of informal settlements. The complexity of the processes involved may require new approaches; generally, mobilizing all available resources is necessary. Partial interventions to deal with the challenges posed by informal settlements may lead to limited and even unintended results. Policy responses should to seek a harmony between carefully chosen policy options, good governance and well-designed legal frameworks.

Guidelines:

1. Complete an analysis and establish a comprehensive understanding of the social, physical and functional processes have brought informal settlements into being in your particular cultural context.

2. Translate strategies and guidelines into your national context.

PRINCIPLE 2

Policies to address informal settlements must be based on the understanding that they are spatial manifestations of social inequality and reflect the complex and multidimensional nature of social inequality. In this context, effective responses should integrate a range of social support measures.

Rationale:

Many recent informal settlements need to be understood in the context of post-socialist transformation, which has led to material dispossession and social distress for much of the population, while enriching only a minority. This extreme situation has posed a major challenge to sustainable economic growth and success in these countries.

Informal settlements are one of the worst spatial manifestations of social inequalities (i.e. uneven wealth redistribution) and have a multidimensional nature. While the diversity of issues underlying the formation of informal settlements has been recognized, policy approaches to informal settlement often address different issues separately and are often purely technical. An understanding that informal settlements reflect a complex concentration of interrelated problems yet are connected to broader societal processes needs to become part of existing policy practices.

There is a need for progressive informal settlement policies that are committed to bringing real change to these places and to peoples' lives. A proactive approach should be based on the understanding of the role that social equality and justice play in ensuring sustainable development. Policies addressing the problems of informal settlements should thus be dedicated to assisting the most disadvantaged people in the most disadvantaged places.

At the same time, it is vital that concrete actions aim to identify the problems in the context of a particular informal settlement in order to allow for better policy integration of local needs. The informal settlement interventions may be insufficient or wrong-headed if certain place-based local factors are not taken into consideration.

Guidelines:

1. Analyse the pattern of uneven wealth redistribution and its impacts in the country and area in question.

2. Understand what processes affect the lives of people in informal settlements and their importance, and confirm your perceptions by listening to people's views regarding opportunities, constraints, intentions, etc.

3. Identify target groups for your policymaking as well as other social groups that are involved or affected.

4. Identify various possible avenues of social support and investment at different levels of government, and allow for continuous dialogue at macro and micro levels.

PRINCIPLE 3

The adoption of an integrated national strategy to address social inequality and unequal spatial redistribution of wealth is fundamental for better policy outcomes for informal settlements.

Rationale:

The complex relationship between social inequality and multiple deprivations within informal settlements poses a great challenge for sustainable development, because different policy goals tend to overlap, e.g. promoting social equality, economic growth and poverty reduction. This demands rapid, innovative and progressive policy responses. National strategies aimed at alleviating poverty should be an overriding goal and a touchstone for effective policy dialogue. Policy responses should be multifaceted, should combine different social fields, should be integrated and should be guided by a clearly-defined national strategy. Economic growth itself cannot achieve redistributive justice without active public interventions in the interests of marginalized groups.

Guidelines:

1. Clearly define short-, intermediate- and long-term goals based on your national context.

2. Adopt joint and cross-sectoral approaches to the policymaking process.

3. Keep your policy perspective open by learning from other countries' experiences and establishing communication with those groups affected.

4. Try to involve a larger community of experts who can help develop innovative solutions.

5. Design clearly defined, result-oriented action plans.

6. Design effective and reflective systems of monitoring and evaluating the implementation and results.

PRINCIPLE 4

A joint and inclusive approach to governance is needed to ensure better results for informal settlements interventions.

Rationale:

Different aspects affecting informal settlements may come from different policy fields. Furthermore, new policy ideas are often poorly communicated and need to be discussed more by a wider range of participants. A limited decision-making process may hamper the programmes' success..

It is necessary to defragment responsibilities and policy responses to deprived areas, and it is essential to allow a range of participants to team up to broaden the perspective on problems and solutions, to design appropriate policy and to support its smooth implementation. Such a joint approach needs to be based on involving more voices in the policymaking process, especially those of affected groups.

Guidelines:

1. Enhance governmental capacity to enable measures supporting marginalized groups for the transformation of informal settlements.

2. Remove unreasonable barriers and ensure that the necessary supporting policies, institutions and processes are in place.

3. Establish a team that will design solutions that encompass different policy fields.

4. Promote inclusive partnerships that allow for effective coordination between key participants.

5. Encourage regular dialogue that is sensitive to both the marginalized people living in informal settlements and to local governments.

6. Create a discourse that in language understandable to the widest community of people.

PRINCIPLE 5

Strategies for informal settlements must be based on a clear understanding of the nature of deprivation in particular informal settlements and should pursue an integrated, people-focused and place-based approach.

Rationale:

Informal settlements concentrate different interrelated problems in a single place. The accumulated problems that manifest themselves in informal settlements significantly shape the life opportunities of the residents and tend to reinforce the vicious circles of social inequality and deprivation. "Problem areas" become juxtaposed with "successful" neighbourhoods. An integrated approach to informal settlements should establish different measures for different places. Such an approach should be based on the principles of sustainable development, social inclusion and social integration.

Guidelines:

1. Understand the pattern of informal settlement formation and define priorities.

2. Establish a single body/coordination framework to bring key players together and establish a dialogue with communities in informal settlements and ensure that they have cross-cutting responsibilities and connections to higher government structures.

3. Ensure basic human rights are guaranteed and basic services are provided.

4. Work together with communities to understand the problems involved and to define community strategies and action plans.

5. Ensure the strategies are delivered.

PRINCIPLE 6

Housing, land and spatial planning policies must always be a key focus for informal settlement policy interventions, and should constitute part of an integrated national strategy to address social inequality and unequal spatial redistribution of wealth

Rationale:

Equal, affordable and secure access to land and housing are fundamental to improving living conditions of the most disadvantaged groups in informal settlements. Effective regulatory tools are thus necessary to achieve such objectives.

The quality of life for these groups can be greatly improved if a new "socially responsible" housing policy is introduced. The housing problem is a multidimensional problem that requires multidimensional solutions. It is thus crucial that effective linkages with other solutions be established. The potential for spatial planning to integrate and coordinate different strategies with land and housing issues must be recognized, and an integrated system of land-use management must be developed to facilitate the decision-making process.

Guidelines:

1. Understand the centrality and multidimensional nature of the housing problem for a given informal settlement.

2. Ensure that housing strategies are well connected and coordinated between different sectors and across different spatial scales.

3. Understand that land reforms, land policies and land management are fundamental to achieving housing objectives.

4. Ensure that land development and land use policies are well connected with the other policies that affect a given informal settlement.

5. Adopt an integrated approach to spatial planning that links physical interventions with positive social and economic outcomes for a given informal settlement.

6. Make use of legal advice and dispute resolution mechanisms regarding land and assets (e.g., out-of-court mediation and arbitration) as important tools to guarantee the protection of land and other rights for disadvantaged people.

7. Enforce land-use regulations, to avoid unsustainable and informal development. Failure to enforce land-use regulations has very large costs to society and the environment. Land administration is an appropriate tool both for securing legal rights and for environmental monitoring.

8. Recording of land uses should be made transparent and information about land use should be available to all real estate market participants.

9. Make sure that land administration and planning are well coordinated. If planning authorities seek to create new land-use patterns without integrating their work with the cadastral system, the implementation of development programmers will almost certainly be delayed and may ultimately fail.

PRINCIPLE 7

It is important to formulate a national strategy for housing that supports marginalized communities.

Rationale:

Given the centrality of housing issues for informal settlements, the link between informal settlement policies and housing policy is of critical importance. The lack of decent housing can be considered as an extreme form of social inequality, and thus allowing access to housing assets in a variety of choices becomes a major goal to narrow the gap between the asset wealth and the asset poor. The need for proactive housing policy to make a real change for the living conditions of the population is also an important precondition for sustainable development.

Currently, the decision-making process is dominated by ideas of an unregulated market in which housing functions are a commodity good. Such thinking marginalises alternative perspectives that recognize housing policy as a key tool for addressing the negative effects of housing segregation. This entails that the State to develop poor-friendly housing policies based on human right principles and that the State commit itself to ensuring equal access to housing for all.

Guidelines:

1. Understand the unequal spatial redistribution of housing wealth and the gap between "asset wealthy" and "asset poor".

2. Consider measures for improving the housing conditions of people in informal settlements as part of a national commitment to ensure the basic right of decent housing for all.

3. Ensure access to housing for the most vulnerable groups.

4. Communicate with people regarding their housing needs and design methods for supporting these needs.

5. Create alternative choices within the same housing market.

6. Create supportive regulatory frameworks that enable the accrual of housing assets.

7. Facilitate access to housing financing for vulnerable groups.

8. Eliminate unreasonable regulations and other urban plans that have negative effects on housing rights and on access to housing of low-income groups.

9. Understand the relationship between housing policy and other policy processes.

PRINCIPLE 8

Informal settlements must be part of a well-designed system of land management committed to providing people with affordable access to serviced land.

Rationale:

Informal settlement transformation must be supported by efficient land management. People in informal settlements often lack or have insecure land rights to support their livelihoods. At the same time, land needs to be considered as a basic human right and a key factor for addressing wealth redistribution. Proactive land policies that create secure and equitable land rights may significantly reduce disparities in asset wealth. They also create further opportunities for low-income people to build their wealth based on land assets and help to ensure social inclusion. It is therefore essential to allow low-income groups to have alternative access to affordable and serviced land.

Guidelines:

1. Ensure that land policy is an integral part of a national strategy to tackle social inequality.

2. Distinguish between social needs and market demands for effective land management.

3. Ensure equitable access, alternative choices and security of different land rights.

4. Consider the opportunities these rights grant citizens in the boader context of their lives.

5. Ensure that land can be used to access financial resources.

6. Ensure supply of serviced land for affordable housing and future urbanization.

7. Develop supportive institutions and legislative frameworks and an integrated cadastre system for land management and property rights registration.

PRINCIPLE 9

There a pro-poor spatial planning system is essential, based on the principles of sustainable development.

Rationale:

Spatial planning can be a powerful tool to combine policies for land use and urban development with other policies and programmes essential for the transformation of deprived places. It can also ensure integration of the different aspects involved (e.g. economic, social and environmental). Spatial planning must be committed to sustainable development, and must recognize and properly address the requirements of particular spatial contexts.

Guidelines:

Analyse informal settlements formations and deprivation as products of the social, physical and functional structures of cities.

Ensure that there is a strong link between local and regional planning strategies.

Establish a dialogue between planning authorities and key players at the level of informal settlements in question.

Strengthen the confidence of marginalized people in the process by also including their voices, and recognizing their stake and their input as necessary for the transformation process.

Consider how land use and development in informal settlements can be connected to other policies important for informal settlement transformation.

Consider how the informal settlement transformation contributes to broader urban and regional strategies, including housing and eliminating social and economic exclusion.

PRINCIPLE 10

Effective policies for informal settlements must consider the development of social capital.[11]

Rationale:

There have been significant recent changes in the role of the State and the relationship between the State and its citizens. New approaches are needed to address the problems of informal settlements. Certain Governments have recently become interested in how social capital in deprived areas can be better linked to their relevant policy interventions.

This new approach requires that Governments change their negative attitude to informal settlements as "illegal" and "distressed" places. Instead, they should focus on various social relations established in informal settlements and find different survival strategies to achieve better outcomes of their interventions. They should not only address the needs of people in informal settlements, but also build on their existing strengths. The integration of social capital into informal settlement strategies strengthens an important link between national and informal settlement levels. The social capital of the most disadvantaged groups must also be enhanced by their taking control over the decision-making processes affecting their future.

Guidelines:

1. Analyse needs, strategies and strengths of the disadvantaged groups in a given informal settlement.

2. Define existing organizations and social networks.

3. Eliminate the social processes that further reinforce deprivation in a given informal settlement.

4. Establish effective communication and cooperation with the people in a given informal settlement.

5. Consider how social capital can further be strengthened.

---

[11] Increasingly, social capital is recognized for its significant contribution to government practices around the world. The concept places greater focus on people and their critical contribution toward economic growth. "Social capital" is described as "networks, norms, trust – that enable participants to act together more effectively to pursue shared objectives" (Putnam 1995: 664–665). There is good evidence on how social capital prevents unlawful actions, contributes to the well-being of communities and economic vitality of places; it also contributes towards better outcomes of various Governments' interventions

PRINCIPLE 11

Knowledge, education, and access to information must be provided.

Rationale:

Building knowledge and capacity becomes an essential element in decision-making in informal settlements. It is also critical for creating an enabling environment. Limited knowledge and capacity and inaccurate information remain substantial barriers to the transformation of informal settlements. The problems of informal settlements require an enhanced capacity on the part of key actors, especially the most disadvantaged groups. All the participants should be able to adapt to changes and to plan, manage and actively participate in the decision-making process. Building knowledge should be collaborative and inclusive.

Guidelines:

1. Assess levels of engagement between government and people in a given informal settlement.

2. Value existing skills and the capacity of people in a given informal settlement as well as the capacity of different public and private organizations involved

3. Evaluate the needs for capacity-building, and decide on the most appropriate action.

4. Develop a communications strategy including, inter alia, networking between different policymakers across different fields and at different levels of government, sharing knowledge using Internet technologies and exchanging practical experience at forums, workshops and community meetings.

5. Consider the most disadvantaged groups as equal partners in knowledge-building.

Annexes

Annex 1 Population Growth and Urbanization

| | Population | | | Urban Population | | | |
| | | Average annual % growth | Density people per square km | Level of urbanization (% population) | Urban population Millions | Annual growth (%) | Capital City |
	Millions 2000	1990-2000	2000	2005	2005	2000-2015	
Western Europe a and North America							
Austria	8	0.5	98	65.8	5.3	0.5	Vienna
Belgium	10	0.3	312	97.3	10	0.0	Brussels
Denmark	5	0.4	126	85.5	4.6	0.1	Copenhagen
Finland	5	0.4	17	60.9	3.1	0.8	Helsinki
France	59	0.4	107	76.7	46.6	0.6	Paris
Germany	82	0.3	235	88.5	73	0.1	Berlin
Greece	11	0.4	82	61.4	6.7	0.4	Athens
Ireland	4	0.8	55	60.4	2.4	1.3	Dublin
Italy	58	0.2	196	67.5	38.7	0	Rome
Luxembourg a	0.44	1.4	169	92.4	0.4	0.7	
Netherlands	16	0.6	469	66.8	10.9	0.2	Hague
Norway	4	0.6	15	80.5	3.7	0.8	Oslo
Portugal	10	0.1	109	55.6	5.6	1.1	Lisbon
Spain	39	0.2	79	76.7	31.5	0.1	Madrid
Sweden	9	0.4	22	83.4	7.4	0.3	Stockholm
Switzerland	7	0.7	182	67.5	4.8	0.5	Zurich
United Kingdom	60	0.4	247	89.2	53.1	0.2	London
Israel	6	2.9	302			1.4	Tel Aviv
Turkey	65	1.5	85			2	Ankara
Western Europe	*458.44*				*307.8*		
Canada	31	1.0	3	81.1	25.9	1.1	Ottawa
United States	282	1.2	31	80.8	242.3	1.0	Washington DC
North America	*313*				*268.2*		
Eastern Europe and the CIS							
Albania	3	0.4	124	45.0	1.4	2.1	Tirana
Bosnia & Herzegovina	4	-1.3	77	45.3	1.9	1.8	
Bulgaria	8	-0.7	74	70.5	5.4	-0.1	Sofia
Croatia	4	-0.7	80	59.9	2.6	0.5	Zagreb
Czech Republic	10	-0.1	133	74.5	7.6	0.0	Prague
Estonia	1	-0.9	34	69.6	0.9	-0.8	Tallinn
Hungary	10	-0.3	109	65.9	6.5	0	Budapest
Latvia	2	-1.0	39	65.9	1.5	-0.7	Riga
Lithuania	4	-0.1	57	66.6	2.3	0	Vilnius
FYROM	2	0.7	80	59.7	1.2		Skopije

	Population			Urban Population			
		Average annual % growth	Density people per square km	Level of urbanization (% population)	Urban population Millions	Annual growth (%)	Capital City
	Millions 2000	1990-2000	2000	2005	2005	2000-2015	
Poland	39	0.1	127	62.0	23.9	0.7	Warsaw
Romania	22	-0.3	97	54.7	12.1	0.3	Bucharest
Serbia & Montenegro	11	0.1	..	52.3	5.5	0.8	Belgrade
Slovakia	5	0.2	112	58.0	3.1	0.6	Bratislava
Slovenia	2	-0.1	99	50.8	1		Ljubliana
Eastern Europe							
Armenia	4	0.8	136	64.1	1.9	1	Yerevan
Azerbaijan	8	1.2	93	49.9	4.2	1.6	Baku
Belarus	10	-0.2	48	71.6	7	0.3	Minsk
Georgia	5	0.0	78	51.5	2.6	0.9	Tbilisi
Kazakhstan	15	-0.9	6	55.9	8.6	0.8	Alma-Ata
Kyrgyzstan				33.7	1.9		
R. Moldova	4	-0.2	129	46.3	1.9	0.7	Chishnau
Russian Federation	146	-0.2	9	73.3	103.7	0.2	Moscow
Tajikistan	6	1.8	45	24.2	1.5	2	
Turkmenistan	5	2.8	10	45.8	2.3	2.2	
Ukraine	50	-0.5	86	67.3	32.2	0	Kiev
Uzbekistan	25	1.8	60	36.4	9.8	1.7	Tashkent
CIS	405				254.5		
World	6065	1.4	47				

Notes: a. Luxembourg, Bosnia & Herzegovina World Development Report (2002) p. 240.

Source: Columns 1-3: World Development Report (2002) pages 232-233
Columns 4-6: State of the World Cities Report (2007)

Annex 2 Urban Population

Country name	1990	1995	2000	2005	2010	2015	2020
Developed regions							
Albania	1 188	1 242	1 306	1 448	1 603	1 762	1 929
Andorra	50	60	61	69	77	86	96
Australia	14 369	15 866	17 375	18 621	19 686	20 628	21 466
Austria	5 083	5 295	5 331	5 343	5 363	5 412	5 497
Belgium	9 606	9 810	9 955	10 076	10 158	10 213	10 257
Bosnia and Herzegovina	1 691	1 400	1 708	1 908	2 051	2 188	2 315
Bulgaria	5 787	5 704	5 569	5 473	5 390	5 300	5 208
Canada	21 214	22 801	24 429	25 930	27 324	28 667	29 958
Croatia	2 617	2 484	2 566	2 637	2 704	2 763	2 815
Czech Republic	7 750	7 716	7 607	7 614	7 634	7 629	7 597
Denmark	4 359	4 440	4 529	4 607	4 672	4 726	4 774
Estonia	1 127	1 010	949	901	861	827	794
Finland	3 063	3 135	3 164	3 180	3 218	3 280	3 362
France	42 015	43 543	44 897	46 554	48 135	49 635	51 062
Germany	67 757	70 633	72 036	73 044	73 729	74 250	74 621
Greece	5 979	6 193	6 552	6 740	6 937	7 139	7 339
Hungary	6 426	6 435	6 406	6 451	6 496	6 531	6 551
Iceland	231	245	261	273	283	292	301
Ireland	2 000	2 090	2 259	2 440	2 612	2 798	2 985
Italy	37 846	38 347	38 677	38 657	38 570	38 428	38 315
Latvia	1 908	1 713	1 586	1 492	1 420	1 369	1 330
Liechtenstein	6	6	7	7	8	9	10
Lithuania	2 528	2 397	2 344	2 266	2 212	2 175	2 151
Luxembourg	326	361	396	429	461	491	521
Malta	315	338	354	366	376	385	392
Monaco	30	32	33	35	36	38	39
Netherlands	8 970	9 553	10 230	10 891	11 470	11 985	12 467
New Zealand	2 848	3 076	3 242	3 381	3 507	3 628	3 748
Norway	3 052	3 197	3 392	3 677	3 901	4 077	4 223
Poland	23 143	23 657	23 846	23 891	24 103	24 444	24 840
Portugal	4 619	4 999	5 312	5 609	5 875	6 109	6 315
Romania	12 350	12 452	12 274	12 154	12 206	12 215	12 178

Country name	1990	1995	2000	2005	2010	2015	2020
Serbia and Montenegro	5 166	5 420	5 444	5 503	5 634	5 802	6 003
Slovakia	2 969	3 047	3 062	3 138	3 228	3 309	3 377
Slovenia	972	1 011	1 011	1 005	1 007	1 016	1 033
Spain	29 615	30 293	31 078	31 573	31 910	32 167	32 315
Sweden	7 112	7 341	7 377	7 421	7 488	7 569	7 668
Switzerland	4 677	4 819	4 849	4 832	4 816	4 815	4 835
FYR of Macedonia	1 103	1 173	1 202	1 239	1 284	1 339	1 398
United Kingdom	50 342	51 202	52 189	53 183	54 151	55 270	56 559
United States	192 551	208 546	225 434	242 305	259 016	275 550	291 865
EURASIA (Countries in CIS)							
Belarus	6 782	6 968	7 003	7 025	7 057	7 088	7 082
Rof Moldova	2 047	2 002	1 961	1 972	2 019	2 104	2 216
Russian Federation	108 830	108 666	106 758	103 730	101 218	99 144	97 201
Ukraine	34 641	34 501	33 363	32 176	31 274	30 575	29 935
Asian countries in CIS							
Armenia	2 372	2 194	2 024	1 950	1 908	1 901	1 908
Azerbaijan	3 864	4 062	4 123	4 253	4 504	4 851	5 280
Georgia	3 006	2 883	2 772	2 587	2 476	2 438	2 428
Kazakhstan	9 586	9 343	8 733	8 594	8 580	8 916	9 297
Kyrgyzstan	1 657	1 644	1 692	1 781	1 914	2 103	2 349
Tajikistan	1 675	1 641	1 568	1 538	1 602	1 770	2 032
Turkmenistan	1 653	1 875	2 080	2 295	2 571	2 911	3 308
Uzbekistan	8 226	8 750	9 282	9 767	10 462	11 379	12 502

Source: UN-HABITAT, 2007

References

Abbott, J. (2002). An Analysis of Informal Settlement Upgrading and Critique of Existing Methodological Approaches. *Habitat International* 26, 303–315.

Angel, S. (2000). *Housing Policy Matters – A Global Analysis*. New York, Oxford University Press.

Atkinson, R. (2000). Combating Social Exclusion in Europe: The New Urban Policy Challenge. *Urban Studies* 37: 5–6, 1037–1055.

Belgrade Urbanism Institute. (2003). *Programme Offering Solutions for the Issue of the Unsafe Settlements in Belgrade*. Belgrade, Belgrade Urbanism Institute.

Belloni, R. (2005) Peace building at the local level: Refugee return to Prijedor. *International Peacekeeping* 12: 3, 434–447.

Besnik, A., K. Lulo and G. Myftiu (2003). *Tirana: The Challenge of Urban Development*. Tirana, CETIS.

Bolay, J. C. (2006) Slums and Urban Development: Questions on Society and Globalization. *European Journal of Development Research* 18: 2, 284–298.

Bruto da Costa, A. and I. Baptista (2001). *Working Together to Prevent Homelessness among Disadvantaged Groups in Portugal*. Brussels, European Observatory on Homelessness.

Carley, M. (2001). Top-down and Bottom-up. The Challenge of Cities in the New Century. M. Carley, P. Jenkins and H. Smith (eds.), *Urban Development & Civil Society. The Role of Communities in Sustainable Cities*. London, Earthscan.

CECODHAS (2007) *Social Housing and Integration of Immigrants in the European Union*. Special edition, autumn 2007. Brussels, CECODHAS-European Social Housing Observatory.

Council of Europe (2002). *Policy Guidelines on Access to Housing for Disadvantaged Categories of Persons*. CS–LO (2001) 31, ECSLO2001.31, Group of Specialists on Access to Housing, Strasbourg, France, Council of Europe.

Council of Europe Development Bank (2004) *Housing in South-Eastern Europe. Solving a Puzzle of Challenges.* Paris, Council of Europe Development Bank.

Deda, L. (2003). The New Housing Market in Tirana. S. Lowe et al. (eds.), *Housing Change in East and Central Europe: Integration or Fragmentation?* Aldershot, United Kingdom, Ashgate Publishing Limited.

Devecigil, P. (2005) "Urban Transformation Projects as a Model to Transform *Gecekondu* Areas in Turkey: The Example of Dikmen Valley, Ankara, *European Journal of Housing Policy* 5: 2, 211–229.

De Soto, H. (2003). *The Mystery of Capital: Why Capitalism Triumphs in the West and Fails Elsewhere.* New York, Basic Books.

Donner, Ch. (2000). Housing Policies in the European Union: Theory and Practice. European Union.

Duncan, J. (2005) From Budapest to Bishkek: Mapping the Root of Poverty Housing. Habitat for Humanity Europe and Central Asia.

Durand–Lasserve, A. (2006) "Informal Settlements and the Millennium Development Goals: Global Policy Debate" Global Urban Development Magazine, vol. 2, issue 1, March.

Durand-Lasserve, H Selod - World Bank's 2007 Urban Research Symposium, 2007 - worldbank.org

European Bank for Reconstruction and Development (2006) Transition Report 2006. London: EBRD

European Commission (2004) The Situation of Roma in an Enlarged European Union. Brussels: European Commission, Directorate–General for Employment and Social Affairs, Unit D3.

Eurostat (2007) Europe in Figures 2006/07. Brussels: European Communities.

Fernandes, E (2004), "Urban Land regulation: State of Knowledge", in Global Urban Poverty, setting the Agenda

Gabriel, B. (2007) "Informal Settlements in SEE – A regional support approach Spatial Information Management toward Legalizing Informal Urban Development". Paper presented at "Informal Settlements – Real Estate Markets Needs Related to Good Land Administration and Planning" FIG Commission 3 Workshop, Athens, March 28–31, 2007

Ioannidis, C.; Psaltis, C. and Posiou, Ch. (2007) "Towards a strategy for suburban informal building control through automatic change detection". Paper presented at "Informal Settlements – Real Estate Markets Needs Related to Good Land

Administration and Planning" FIG Commission 3 Workshop, Athens, Greece, March 28–31, 2007

Jahn, A. and Straubhaar, T. (1999) "A survey of the economics of illegal immigration", in Baldwin–Edwards, M. and Arango, J. (eds.), Immigrants in the Informal Economy in Southern Europe, London, Frank Cass.

Hegedüs, J., S. Mayo and I. Tosics. 1996. "Transition of the Housing Sector in the East Central European Countries'. Review of Urban & Regional Development Studies. No. 8, pp.101–136.

Heitkamp, Thorsten (2000). "The integration of unplanned towns in the periphery of Madrid: The case of Fuenlabrada," Habitat International 24, pp.213–220.

International Finance Corporation (IFC) (2006) Central Asia Housing Finance Gap Analysis. Washington DC: IFC and the World Bank Group.

Internal Displacement Monitoring Centre (IDMC)(2007)Global Monitoring Project, http://www.internal–displacement.org/, accessed 26October 2007.

Joint Center for Housing Studies of Harvard University (JCHS) (2007) The State of the Nation's Housing 2007. Harvard: JCHS.

Kreibich, V. (2000). "Self–help planning of migrants in Rome and Madrid," Habitat International v.24, pp. 201–211.

Leckie, S. (2002) Regional Housing Issues Profile, Implementing Housing Rights in South East Europe, Nairobi: UN–Habitat

Lux, M. (ed). (2003). Housing Policy: An End or a New Beginning. Budapest: Local Government Initiative, Open Society Institute.

Mandič, S. (2006) Fourth Review of Policies on Homelessness in Europe. Brussels: FEANTSA.

Milic.V, Petovar. K, Colic. R, (2004) Ministerial conference on Informal Settlements in SEE, Vienna. Serbian National Perspective in Informal Settlements.

Ministry of Capital Investment Republic of Serbia, The Urban and spatial Planning and Housing Department. Report of urban development and illegal construction in the Republic of Serbia.

Ministry of Infrastructure of the Italian Republic & Federcasa (MoIR) (2007). Housing Statistics in the European Union, 2006/07. Rome: MoIR.

Ministry of Economy Republic of Azerbaijan(2003) State Programme on Poverty Reduction and Economic Development, 2003–2005. Baku: Ministry of Economy.

Müller, Y and Lješkovič, S. (2007) "Illegal construction in Montenegro", Paper presented at "Informal Settlements – Real Estate Markets Needs Related to Good Land Administration and Planning" FIG Commission 3 Workshop, Athens, Greece, March 28–31, 2007.

Municipality of Tirana. (2004). "The Development of Informal Settlements in Tirana" Presented at the Ministerial Conference on Informal Settlements in South Eastern Europe 28 Sept – 01 Oct 2004. Retrieved on November 16th, 2007 from http://www.stabilitypact.org/humi/040928–presentations/tirana.pdf. OSCE (2006) Report on Roma Informal Settlements in Bosnia and Herzegovina. Sarajevo: OSCE– Mission to Bosnia and Herzegovina, http://www.cohre.org/view_page.php?page_id=237, accessed on November 15, 2007.

Ozer. G.; Vardar, A. and Nazım, M. (2007) "Unplanned Settlements within the context of Urbanization Process of Turkey". Paper presented at "Informal Settlements – Real Estate Markets Needs Related to Good Land Administration and Planning" FIG Commission 3 Workshop, Athens, Greece, March 28–31, 2007.

Payne, G., & Majale, M. (2004). The Urban Housing Manual: making regulatory frameworks work for the poor. London: Earthscan.

Potsiou C and Ioannidis C. (2006). "Informal Settlements in Greece: The Mystery of Missing Information and the Difficulty of Their Integration into a Legal Framework, Promoting Land Administration and Good Governance" paper presented at 5th FIG Regional Conference, Accra, Ghana, March 8–11, 2006.

Potsiou 1, C. (2007). "Informal Development: It can be an Asset", Geoinformatics, volume 10, N. o2, March 2007.

Potsiou 2, C. (2007). "Workshop on Spatial Information Management toward Legalizing Informal Urban Development and Informal Settlements–Real Estate Market Needs for Good Land Administration and Planning:Workshop report", SaLIS Journal, vol.67,No2, 2007, pp. 91–96

Potsiou. C. Mueller, H. (2007) "Comparative Thoughts on German and Hellenic Urban Planning and Property Registration ". Paper presented at "Informal Settlements – Real Estate Markets Needs Related to Good Land Administration and Planning" FIG Commission 3 Workshop, Athens, Greece, March 28–31, 2007

Potsiou, C., Dimitriadi, K, (2008) "Tools for Legal Integration and Regeneration of Informal Development in Greece: A Research Study in the Municipality of Keratea", SaLIS Journal, Vol.68, No2, 2008, pp. 103–118

Putnam, Robert D. (1995), "Bowling Alone: America's Declining Social Capital", Journal of Democracy - Volume 6, Number 1, January 1995

Registra, Analystas and Imantra (2005) Housing Finance in Croatia, report for IFC, Washington DC.

Royal Institution of Chartered Surveyors (RICS) (2007) European Housing Review 2007. London: RICS.

Soaita, A.(2007)"The new housing developments in Romania: Challenges and resident Involvement". Paper presented at the European Network for Housing Research Conference, Rotterdam, 21–25 June, 2007

Struyk, R. (ed) (2000). Homeownership and Housing Finance Policy in the Former Soviet Bloc: Costly Populism. Washington D.C: Urban Institute Press.

Tsenkova, S. (2003). "Housing Policy Matters: The Reform Path in Central and Eastern Europe: Policy Convergence?" in Tsenkova, S. and S. Lowe (eds) Housing Change in Central and Eastern Europe: Integration or Fragmentation. Aldershot: Ashgate Publishing Limited, pp.193–205.

_____ (2005) Trends and Progress in Housing Reforms in South East Europe. Paris: Council of Europe Development Bank.

_____ (2006) Beyond Transitions: Understanding Urban change in post–socialist Cities. In Tsenkova, S. and Nedovic–Budic, Z. (eds) The Urban Mosaic of Post–socialist Europe, Heidelberg: Springer–Verlag

_____ (2007) Informal Settlements in the UNECE Region. Survey Results. Geneva: UNECE.

Turró, M: Field, B and Carbonaro, G. (2007) "A Changing Scenario for European Support of Urban Renewal and Development: The first steps of JESSICA". Informationen zur Raumentwicklung, Heft 9.2007 573.

United Nations Economic Commission for Europe (UNECE) (2001) Land Administration Review: Georgia. Geneva: United Nations Economic Commission for Europe.

_____ (2002) Country Profiles on Housing: Albania. Geneva: United Nations Economic Commission for Europe.

_____ (2003) Country Profiles on Housing: Armenia. Geneva: United Nations Economic Commission for Europe.

_____ (2004) Sustainable Development of Human Settlements in the UNECE region: progress and challenges.

_____ (2005) Country Profiles on Housing: Serbia and Montenegro. Geneva: United Nations Economic Commission for Europe.

_____ (2006) Country Profile on the Housing Sector, Serbia and Montenegro

_____ (2007a) Country Profiles on Housing: Georgia. Geneva: United Nations Economic Commission for Europe.

_____ (2007b). UNECE Countries in Figures 2007. `New York and Geneva: United Nations Economic Commission for Europe.

_____ (2009) – Country Profile on Housing and Land sector in Kyrgyz Republic. Committee on Housing and Land Management.

United Nations Human Settlements Programme (UN–HABITAT) (2001), Declaration on Cities and Other Human Settlements in the New Millennium

_____ (2002a),Dialogue on urban cultures: globalization and culture in an urbanizing world

_____ (2003). Global Report on Human Settlements 2003. The Challenge of Slums. London: Earthscan.

_____ (2004) Pro Poor land Management. Integrating Slums into City Planning Approaches. Nairobi: UN–HABITAT.

_____ (2005a) Global Report on Human Settlements 2005. London: Earthscan.

_____ (2005b) Housing and Property Rights: Bosnia and Herzegovina, Croatia, Serbia and Montenegro. Nairobi: UN–HABITAT.

_____ (2006) Four Strategic Themes for the Housing Policy in Serbia. Belgrade: Settlement and Integration of Refugee Programme in Serbia (SIRP).

_____ (2007) State of the World Cities Report 2006/07. London: Earthscan.

Vienna Declaration (2004). "Annex B: Vienna Declaration" in Report: Ministerial Conference on Informal Settlements in South EasternEurope, OSCE Hofburg in Vienna, 28 Sep – 01 Oct 2004. Retrieved on October 25th, 2007 from http://www.stabilitypact.org/humi/041001–conference.html

Wegelin, E. (2003) Refugee–related Housing Issues in selected SEE Countries presented at CEB/WB Housing Conference, Paris, April 2003.

Williams, R. (2007) "The contemporary right to property restitution in the contest of transitional justice" Bosnia case. International Centre for Transitional Justice, Occasional Paper Series.

The World Bank (2001) Upgrading Urban Communities: A Resource Framework. Washington, D.C.: The World Bank , CD ROM

_____ .(2002) Transition – the First Ten Years: Analysis and Lessons for Eastern Europe and the Former Soviet Union. Washington, D.C.: The World Bank. Europe and Central Asia Regional Department (ECA).

_____ .(2005) Meeting the Millennium Development Goals in Europe and Central Asia. Background Reports. Washington DC: The World Bank

_____ (2007) "World Bank Responses to the Problem of Informal Development: Current Projects and Future Action" . Paper presented at "Informal Settlements – Real Estate Markets Needs Related to Good Land Administration and Planning" FIG Commission 3 Workshop, Athens, Greece, March 28–31, 2007

Zrnic, A. (2009) "Nova Orlovaca, Informal Settlements Case Study". NALAS Network of Association of Local Authorities of South–East Europe.